THE LITTLE BOOK OF

BIG SCALE

THE LITTLE BOOK OF

BIG SCALE

5 COUNTERINTUITIVE PRACTICES
FOR EXPONENTIAL GROWTH

JOHN HITTLER

HOUNDSTOOTH
PRESS

THE LITTLE BOOK OF BIG SCALE
5 Counterintuitive Practices for Exponential Growth

ISBN   978-1-5445-3514-2   *Hardcover*

978-1-5445-3513-5   *Paperback*

978-1-5445-3515-9   *Ebook*

CONTENTS

This book is dedicated to the courageous entrepreneurs who continue to defy the odds, take on big challenges, and play in the hard-scrabble game of business. Win or lose, you inspire your teams and customers with your passion, vision, and dedication to your craft.

WHY A BOOK ABOUT SCALING NOW?

"Winning isn't everything; it's the only thing."

—VINCE LOMBARDI

Venture Capitalists, entrepreneurs, private equity firms, and small retail shoe store owners have one thing in common: they would like their endeavors to result in higher growth and profits.

More specifically, they seek profitability with the prospect for continually higher growth in revenue, net margin, employee headcount, or user acquisitions—fast growth nonetheless. The Holy Grail is *scaling*, where all investors and most employees benefit greatly.

Two premises exist when discussing the idea of scaling. The first is that scaling is simply a form of change—from what you are doing currently (or more precisely, *think you are doing*) to growing 50% faster than your industry, year over year. And here's the rub: If you're copying what you think a competitor or friend is doing to scale, you're likely to fail. After all, you are not Elon Musk or Jeff Bezos, and your company is not built like theirs.

Your scaling story will need a frame—built and nourished by you and your team, customized to your specific talents, products, people, and customers. As a rule, the vast majority of humans prefer predictability and stability. Your own scaling story will depend upon you leaning into almost constant uncertainty. It often will look a bit counterintuitive, since your explanation after the fact will sound simple and easy to others. In reality, your path will be anything but what others can easily duplicate. Much like you cannot simply copy a successful model (otherwise, everyone would scale), your journey will be uniquely yours to enjoy.

The second premise is that scaling exists fundamentally as a leadership activity rather than a sales activity. If not, every company would simply focus on doubling sales every year and producing twice as much product. If scaling were that logical or linear, we would all issue shares for our upcoming IPOs. Scaling involves the courage to charge into an unexplored niche, or even a gigantically inefficient marketplace. Take banking in the past decade. Multiple companies have taken a large chunk of the banking business away from traditional players. These companies are now household names: PayPal,

Venmo, Revolut, Chime, Box, Plaid, Brex—the list is long. All of that growth and value creation started as declarations from leaders. Those declarations came from two fundamental things: 1) a complaint about what was lacking, and 2) a vision of what might be possible.

Leadership jump-starts scaling (or prevents it), and that leadership generally works best with the CEO out in front of the team.

SO WHY NOW?

I wrote *The Little Book of Big Scale* for those willing to take on inherent risks, invest a sizable chunk of capital, and then work insanely long and hard hours to create a success. Call them disrupters, entrepreneurs, or simply innovators. Whatever the name, they deserve all of the prizes for effectively scaling. Those fortunate enough earn the accolades, notoriety, and also the check that usually accompanies scaling. For CEOs, the new reputation as a successful entrepreneur is often the most prized trophy, as they join an exclusive club.

But here's the conundrum. For every company that hires well, develops an effective culture, and designs a service or product with promise, there are nine companies that fail using the exact same recipe. How do you tell the differences between the one-in-ten who succeeds and the nine-in-ten who do not? Postmortems can help, but the tendency is to shrug your shoulders and just call it random luck. Certainly good fortune and timing can play a part, but there are usually equal amounts of inopportune timing and poor luck too, so what really makes a success in one company but not a similar success in another?

This book explores some of the counterintuitive, not so obvious, and predictably useful rules and practices that scale effectively over time, regardless of product, service, industry, culture, or size. These practices were drawn from CEOs successful at scaling. I break down their practices into simple form such that you can use them in your company—with some basic customization of your own.

This book offers notions and ideas that most companies do *not* employ, strategies that are often just the opposite of what most companies do. The key is that the counterintuitive practices discussed are tied purposely to scaling, nothing else. Some practices function better with a culture-first bias, and others work better when companies focus primarily on hiring talent devoid of the cultural implications. I also introduce structure, separate from culture and talent, as an often-overlooked part of rapid growth. The practices presented in this book show effectiveness at every size, and the CEOs explain how to scale the practices from "garage-band-sized" companies to large companies pursuing IPOs. Most importantly, instructions are provided on how you can implement and customize these counterintuitive practices into your company.

You'll meet the CEOs who are successfully scaling, how they are doing it, and, perhaps most importantly, why they choose to go against the herd, or *counterintuitively* create scale. Considering the historical one-in-a-million chance of success following the existing "recipe," taking a counterintuitive approach increases your chances of scaling and actually makes great statistical sense. If not, the traditional approach would yield a much higher success rate and become the easier bet to place.

IS THERE A RECIPE?

What if companies could dramatically increase their odds of success simply by engaging counterintuitive practices rather than following (much) more popular notions...that fail at a very high rate?

Succeeding often occurs in business in counterintuitive ways. Just to play in the entrepreneurial game most likely will take you four or five years, marked by very long hours, sleepless nights, stress, and the absence from some key family events. So then, why not win the game, or at least dramatically increase your chances?

After having founded nine companies and one charitable foundation myself, seven of the nine companies eventually (mercifully, in some cases) failed. Still, people console me that two for nine is a better success rate than most billionaire venture capitalists produce. "Coming close" and eventually failing hurts, especially if someone else beats you to the win. But failures also provide great lessons on what to avoid.

WHAT ARE THE "SECRETS" TO SCALING?

Watching some companies scale so elegantly, one would think that scaling is, well...easy. Just follow some simple rules, hire the right people, build a great culture and an innovative product, and then work really hard. Could it really be that easy? Or that difficult? More like mysterious, or what we call counterintuitive.

The approaches, the methodologies, and the practices presented in this book can sound simple and obvious, but with one realization: you will have never thought of most of the practices before! Why is this? In our interviews, the creators of the practices simply view them as obvious and useful rather than noteworthy. The practices are helpful to solve problems of all kinds. The entrepreneurs are focusing on building companies, not becoming noted experts for innovating a management or leadership practice that scales. They'd just as soon leave that to university researchers in noted business schools.

> *Once you understand each concept, and accept that the approach alters what you are doing currently, then almost all of the practices can be implemented and customized for your specific team, customer, or product.*

That's what I mean by *counterintuitive*.

For a sneak preview, consider these two highly effective practices, both provocative (read: controversial), and one of which is clearly NOT followed by most companies, despite overwhelming evidence that it works.

Start with the notion that **hiring for talent *exclusively* over any sort of cultural fit** scales significantly faster than does the reverse. I'll show you exactly how and why in Chapter 8. Many companies deploy the practice with predictable results for their growth, but also with positive impact to their cultures. If you deploy just this one counterintuitive practice, you dramatically increase your chances to scale, as talent beats out culture fit by a three-to-one pace when scaling. Ironically, most CEOs interviewed held a very strong bias that their culture is the primary catalyst to building a scaling company. You can scale either with culture fit or talent as your primary lever. If you were to place a bet in Vegas, pick talent and allow the culture to follow.

A second highly effective practice involves **holding only *one* core value, spoken in the form of a directive.** For example, instead of holding "honesty" as your highest core value, replace it with "Tell the entire truth up front, regardless of the outcome!" This singular form of command, or directive, scales a company much faster than multiple core values for two reasons: 1) It is spoken only in the form of a command (as in, you have to obey it to belong); and 2) It stands as the singular or primary directive in the entire company.

In short, most companies pit their values against each other daily, in ways that team members either ignore or have to gain perspective and permission from managers before deciding which direction to take. Limited to only *one* core value, companies have to "get it right" (the value, that is) since there are no "back-up" values. That focuses attention and allows for anyone in the company to make much more effective and quicker decisions, at almost any time. Creating this one focus ensures speed, reduction in meetings, and redundancy found in most companies. We showcase this concept in depth in Chapter 6 and outline several examples from some of the CEOs who are utilizing it and scaling. You'll learn to design and implement your own. It's one of those concepts that qualifies as *simple but not easy*.

We found this practice works best at a certain head count, namely 50+. That makes sense, as core values tend to be organic at the start of any company, before complexity starts to set in. A singular core value cleans up practices that have organically outgrown their usefulness. The companies we found who are using this one-core-directive approach invigorated and dramatically accelerated their growth once they deployed the practice.

It scales. That's all we concern ourselves with here.

THE PROCESS AND RESEARCH

My approach when writing this book was to find *counterintuitive* methodologies, beliefs, and practices. My research included interviewing more than 275 successful CEOs, many of them on multiple occasions, to gather information that could not be garnered from surveys and financial records alone. Those interviews created only *possible* theories, which we then challenged, vetted, and eventually confirmed or, in most cases, dismissed. Like the high percentage of companies that eventually fail, so did most of the initial theories. Many practices initially sounded promising but fell apart under scrutiny. They simply did not produce faster or higher growth. Some worked great but only for one industry or company size.

I was looking for practices that work across most or all industries, physical or intangible products or services, and various company sizes. The practice used for 50 employees or $3M in revenue had to play just as well, albeit a bit differently, when employed for 2,500 employees or $50M in revenue. I gave priority to practices that increased the rate of scaling at a higher revenue or headcount, as they added more value.

As a backdrop, the interviews were spread over publicly traded companies, many "up and comers," a handful of family businesses, non-profits, and almost any industry and product segment you could imagine. For clarity, I defined scaling as *"growing 50% faster than does your industry, year after year."* This effectively eliminated one-hit wonders who had a good year or two and then fell apart.

I coach CEOs, mostly in fast-growing companies. *The Little Book of Big Scale* started with several of my own theories about who scales better and why, and the only theory that was well-established prior to interviewing and writing it was that **CEOs and leadership teams scale businesses.** In short, if your CEO and Jeff Bezos swapped companies, your current company would scale much faster with Bezos at the helm. Bezos' companies (Amazon, Blue Origin, and anything else he might be running) would predictably slow their scaling over time if you suddenly started to run them.

That theory held up pretty well in the interviews. In short, idiots and assholes generally cannot and do not scale, although Enron and WeWork prove that they sometimes can...at least for a while. Talented leaders hold a better chance, though they still face very tough odds. Over time, however, the safest bet is on talent in the leadership ranks as the primary factor to ensure scale.

The rest of the theories up for debate in this book—and they are just that, theories—came from the CEOs themselves. What do they do daily to drive rapid growth? How much time do they invest in creating and developing a culture? How do they attract and retain the best talent? Does the source of their investment money make any difference at all? How much time and money do they invest in their own individual growth? I was both surprised and pleased with the incredible depth and wisdom of the CEOs. You will meet many of these interesting and diverse people, with even more interesting and diverse companies, in the chapters to follow.

The type of research *not* included in this book is massive, decade-long, university-type studies or experiments often conducted in prestigious business schools. I used interviewing as my key research tool, and as such, the book relies on retelling—stories, ideas, practices, etc. We checked metrics only after we liked a counterintuitive concept or practice. Novelty and popularity were not criteria for inclusion.

Our simple yardstick for vetting was demonstrable success. We vetted for results, always. Even if we really thought an idea held promise, if it didn't produce results—meaning, it did not scale a company—in our eyes, it did not count. If the great idea was offered by a CEO whose company was not yet scaling, but we were able to find it working in companies that were, then we happily included the idea, as there was evidence elsewhere.

All this to say, there are not volumes of data, statistics, or metrics for the reader, but instead amazing stories from CEOs who are "walking the walk." Those hours of interviews provided invaluable data, limited only by the creativity and values of the CEOs who developed and deployed the methods discussed.

Finally, know that the rules and practices contained herein are for scaling companies and those who want to increase their pace of growth. If you are looking for safety or stability, this book may not be for you.

STRUCTURE OF THE BOOK

I use two phrases throughout this book that I need to explain. The first is "beauty contest for idiots," a term used by one of the CEOs I interviewed. It refers to ideas and concepts that clearly do not scale but which founders, CEOs, and entire organizations insist do. As my grandpa used to remind my siblings and me, "Never argue with a crazy person, since no one can tell who is who."

The second phrase is "two-day-old sushi," which represents a demonstrably bad idea that somehow is utilized regardless of the overwhelming evidence against it. Not surprisingly, you might feel a bit queasy when you hear about these, since two-day-old sushi is only ever bought at a significantly discounted price. Eat those ideas at your own risk.

Every chapter ends with a list of key learning points. In chapters where a tool or counterintuitive (best) practice is discussed, I insert a quick outline on a separate page following the chapter. I also list rules at the end of some chapters; I leave it to you to implement the rules or not.

If you're ready to consider your own company rules and practices, let's start scaling! That process starts with some ground rules for entrepreneurs, leaders, and CEOs who want to grow faster and in simpler fashion than previously experienced.

PART 1

GROUND RULES FOR SCALING... OR LIFE

CHAPTER 1

THE REALITY ABOUT WORK-LIFE BALANCE

"There is no such thing as work-life balance. There are work-life choices, and you make them, and they have consequences."

—JACK WELCH

WHETHER YOU WORK FULL-TIME, PART-TIME, OR NOT AT ALL, you decide every day how to best invest your time, energy, and talents. Do you exercise daily as a high priority? Eat dinner with your family each night? Drive results as a key member of your team at work?

Your life. Your choices.

Steven Freidkin signed up for a company founder role that is hectic, demands long hours, holds big challenges, and, far too often, does not have enough resources. The contract never pointed out any of this, but he knew what to expect when he ventured into the entrepreneurial game. It was a bit of a David versus Goliath challenge, as are most new ventures. His contract was clear to him, since the entrepreneurial game has been his only game for a long time. After starting his first successful IT company in his teens, Steven now runs Ntiva, a full-service technology firm that provides businesses with advanced technology expertise and support, including managed IT services, strategic consulting, cloud services, cybersecurity, and telecom solutions.

Meanwhile, Steven has a full life: a wife, five kids, hobbies, and friends. You might think Steven had only some of those blessings at times, given the rigors of running a growing company. After all, he gets only as many hours each day as non-entrepreneurs. His integration of what matters most to him rests as the key, because how do you choose between your marriage, work, kids, and health? In the end, something has to give. There are rarely enough hours in the week to do everything. So how, then, does Steven maintain or engage in any sort of "work-life balance"?

The short answer: he doesn't. Steven *integrates* rather than balances.

If you are playing in a fast-growth or scaling game, you too have choices to make, and one of them does not include work-life balance...whatever the heck that is. Take it from Steven: "To work at Ntiva in a senior position, you have to want to work to live, not live to work. The latter group mostly opts out. In the end, we exist to grow people, not guarantee any sort of mythical balance."

Steven is wise enough as the CEO of a rapidly scaling company to know that "all good ideas come from individuals, not from the CEO." If that weren't true, he would never get a day off. Part of the way he enjoys a great life is by growing people and allowing them to figure out how to contribute to growing a great company.

Because of that simple belief, the idea of having a life outside of work does not come up much at Ntiva. Fulfilling work is simply one part of living a great life. Who would want to limit that advantage?

ADDRESSING THE ACTUAL CHALLENGE

There exists a myth in our culture that has people feeling as if they need to cultivate, perfect, and then pursue what people call work-life balance.

Is there really such a thing? More importantly, even if there were, *why on earth would you ever want that?* Much like Steven, you are in full charge of figuring out how to have a great life, and work is simply one piece of that equation, much like great relationships, ample sleep, hobbies, or suitable exercise. Why limit any of these, or worse yet, attempt to balance them in some formulaic way?

Assuming that you work way too much and it negatively impacts your relationships, your health, your hobbies, your sleep—you name it—then yes, reining in your overly active work schedule seems an appropriate and healthy move. That same rule applies to eating too much unhealthy food, watching too much trash TV, or allowing yourself to go three weeks without changing out of your Saturday morning sweats.

Just ask people who got a six-month severance if they enjoyed the total freedom to "balance" their lives with some long-needed rest and rejuvenation during their time off. The bulk of them will report they felt a nagging need to find their next gig before they could enjoy time off. When they worked too much, they craved free time. With ample, paid free time, they worried about finding meaningful work. No balance.

In the end, I suggest you and I are solving the wrong problem. In coaching clients who work too much, most are either incompetent or do not prioritize well enough to fulfill the responsibilities of their roles. Their lack of "balancing their work hours" is a choice connected to very different challenges.

If you work too much, am I calling you incompetent? Strong words, indeed. When I say "incompetent," I simply mean it in the same way as one might be incompetent at baking French pastries or speaking a foreign language. You simply do not know how to work efficiently rather than lack the intelligence to do so. Your ability to perform your work role simply takes an inordinately long amount of time to leave sufficient margin for other activities.

Your calendar and bank statement highlight where you are investing your time and energy. What takes priority, your health or your next video call with the team? You alone are in charge of that equation rather than anyone else. Balance seems like an inappropriate context.

However experienced you are in your career, you can still be incompetent at accomplishing what you need to do in an efficient and appropriate amount of time. The work is never anything but the work. You might complete it successfully in one way, and I might complete it completely differently. If both practices are acceptable, whose practice leaves more time for other activities?

Some common versions of "incompetence" that lead to an inefficient reliance on time (rather than on skill or delegation) in order to create results are:

Micromanagement—If you are a leader or manager who micromanages, the constant message you send to your team is that you need to know everything in order to do your own job and feel comfortable or confident. Micromanagement adds lots of hours to all schedules (yours and theirs) because two people—the person with the actual functional responsibility and the person watching over him or her—are spending time on the same task. You will end up "out of balance" at work because you spend time doing things others are already paid to do. As Steven realized, "All ideas come from people *other than* the CEO." Might that hold true at almost all scaling companies? If not, they will quickly stall in their growth. Not micromanaging also allows Steven to enjoy dinner with his family, take weekends off, and maintain good health.

Reliance on standing meetings—On average, professionals spend 23 hours/week in (scheduled) meetings! If you consider a 40-hour work week (unheard of in a growing company), that's more than half of your time already allotted to meetings, most of which are scheduled for an hour. Even if you work 60 hours/week, the idea that you should be in 23 hours of required meetings each week speaks to the redundancy or lack of usefulness of those meetings.

When pressed as to why meetings are scheduled for an hour, employees came back with a simple answer: because it works well on calendaring systems like Outlook! What if each meeting were scheduled for only 30 minutes? Which meetings could be more effective if only 15 minutes long? Name the five meetings that you could eliminate today (at least for yourself) and take back some ill-spent hours. What if you were to become super discerning about exactly which meetings require your talent and input, and only then would you attend? What if you did not attend some meetings that you have in the past? Could you instead get a simple debrief of what occurred?

A drive to **work longer hours than everyone else.** Very oddly, many cultures include an unwritten and unspoken rule that "if you would like to advance, you had better arrive before the boss and leave after the boss." If your teams work a perverse number of hours each week, then you end up in a difficult predicament: work insanely long hours as the leader, or limit possible advancement for both yourself and other ambitious team members. Many CEOs "live at the office," and that sets up the entire organization for burnout and exhaustion. What might occur if the CEO or team leader left early to coach her child's soccer team?

A third option exists—changing cultures to a meritocracy, where you are revered for the results you create rather than receiving a "badge of honor" for staying really late every day. Steven Freidkin's team is compensated, noticed, and acknowledged for the work they actually do rather than how many hours they are at work. No one compares the hours spent.

WHY WOULD YOU EVER WANT WORK-LIFE BALANCE?

When considering how to pursue a healthy work-life balance, could it be that we are pursuing the wrong outcome? Just like children model actions from their parents, so too do team members model behavior after the leaders of any company.

Let's say you want to monitor your calories and the source of your food (for example, eating organic, hormone-free, low-calorie, or vegan), all in the proper portions. If you could eat only extremely healthy, low-fat, delicious food every night for dinner, would you feel the need to "balance" that with nights where you eat nutritionally deficient "gut fill" food? Hmm...if dinner every night included organic, delicious, aesthetically pleasing meals, my guess is that you would naturally run toward the healthy and delicious choices every time, without any need for the "balance" that sweets, alcohol, pizza, or fried foods add to the equation.

Let's also say you want to adopt a learning and growth platform that exposes you to all types of new opportunities to expand your skills, interests, and hobbies. That would be quite fun. Your capability as a leader would improve while you were learning and growing. Would you then require couch-potato weekends to watch *The Real Housewives of Your Neighborhood* to "balance" the abundance of compelling learning and growth?

Assuming that we need or want balance essentially addresses a corrective strategy for the wrong outcome. After all, when was the last time your Board members had a one-on-one with you, as the CEO, about your personal activities that were way out of balance when compared to your time and effort invested at work? It rarely happens. Those absentee leaders cannot lead a scaling organization, as there is simply too much interesting and pressing work to take on. It does not, however, require 80-hour weeks to achieve.

What if instead, you simply engaged only in activities where you held passion, skill, interest, and, most importantly, energy? In short, you hold one filter for both professional and personal activities? If this were the case, what would you pursue more of? More activities with your family, your kids, your hobbies... or fewer? Would you dive into your work more, because work feels like play, or are you running a mythical playbook required to advance in the organization?

A friend and client in Chicago (he asked for confidentiality) holds a simple life philosophy he employs every day: *Have fun at everything I do, or enjoy the exit!*

When I asked him how that looks when he goes to a boring or contentious Thanksgiving dinner, he did not flinch: "My one brother and sister-in-law host every fourth year, and it's always horrible: divisive politics, too much drinking, arguments, the works! My wife and I always have a Plan B ready, and if drunk relatives start the poor behaviors, we simply exit and go to the movies, or another friend's home."

Mind you, this friend deploys his philosophy in his profession in a similar manner. He ranks in the top 1% of producers in his industry. Same rule: have fun or exit, whether professional or personal. What's your guess on whether he attends the "mandatory" Monday morning office meeting? Is his life in balance? No way. He plays far too much tennis, because he loves it. He enjoys his boat and at least three "once-in-a-lifetime" trips *every year*. He also pursues the largest deals in his industry and wins way more than any other top player. He might agree that he is completely out of balance....and loving every minute!

Life is too short to participate in activities that suck the life out of you. If your work consists of one of those activities, the responsibility to transform your relationship with work is yours alone! If you work long hours in order to avoid the loneliness, conflict, or unhappiness at home, the responsibility rests with you to change your home life. Imbalance is simply not the root cause of unhappiness.

Either way, your contribution to helping your team at work diminishes if you dislike or simply endure your work every day. Additionally, you'll be only partially effective if you are not investing enough time with people and activities outside of work. In the end, it's up to you alone to choose what you do.

Scaling does not allow or disallow work-life balance. Keeping your health, sanity, and interest in any aspect of your life requires that you love what you do...and resign from the unnecessary or soul-sucking activities you have agreed to do.

MAKE YOUR SIMPLE DECLARATIONS!

Declarations rest as the simplest form of creation. Think of the first verses in the Bible, such as "Let there be light." All are declarations of creation. Sports teams declare championships into existence and then create from there. CEOs do the same, declaring objectives, outcomes, and deadlines into existence.

> *Rarely do we make progress without some form of a declaration of an intention, a goal, or a concrete plan.*

What if you redesigned some simple declarations about the passion and enjoyment of your work, as well as declarations about the rest of your life? What might your life look like if you absolutely loved your daily work and also loved the people you work with? Would you need to balance it, or limit it?

How about the rest of your life? If you make simple declarations that redesign aspects you do not like, again, you will have no need to balance your life with your work. You simply enjoy every moment, whether working or hanging out with people you love (while not working)!

Solve the correct challenge: *love* what you do (work or not), without any need for balancing the time invested. Do only those things you love with people you want to be around. If that were the only requirement to address having a great life, it would then address the more achievable goal: "to work to live rather than live to work," as Steven Freidkin professes.

Done well, this strategy will likely result in a much richer list of activities and people you play with, with no sense of missing out on much. Start with some of these simple declarations as a base:

- I love what I do! (Notice that the work does not change, only your choice to love it.)

- I work with great, talented people.

- I enjoy healthy activities with my family.

- I eat dinner at home with my spouse.

- I spend time with friends regularly.

- I sleep eight hours every night.

You get the idea. None of these really has anything to do with work. They are simply marching orders of your own creation that redesign how you create the life you would like rather than succumbing to the idea of work being the enemy, or the unbalanced aspect of your life.

In the end, scaling is not for the faint-hearted. Better enjoy it, or else go do something you love much more. Companies where the "work feels like play" hold a marked advantage (11% increase in liquidity events) over those where work simply seems never-ending. Scaling will be absolutely challenging, especially if you expect it to be rewarding. It should feel like a great challenge to engage your full talents—a bit like a kid taking on a super complex Lego set or a one-thousand-piece puzzle. Yes, it's hard, but in a manner that engulfs your interest.

If work is simply an exercise in long hours, the loss of sleep alone leads to mistakes, as exhausted people—leaders or not— miss things. Go play at a place that engages your talents at their highest levels.

Start with that as your first declaration.

> **Two-Day-Old Sushi:** Creating new declarations that have negative language. For example, "I will never work for a jerk." A fresher idea: State what you want, not what you do not want. For example, much more powerful is, "I work with people I respect."

Rule #1: There is no such thing as work-balance.

KEY LEARNING POINTS

1. A "work-life imbalance" is improperly named. Work-life integration describes the actual game.

2. The biggest causes of working too much are micromanaging, excessive meetings, and attempting to keep up with other people's ideas for how long to work.

3. Improving integration of life with work requires new, simple declarations. Those declarations should always be spoken in the affirmative, that is, what you *will* do, as opposed to what you will no longer do.

If you're ready, let's now firm up your position in your market.

CHAPTER 2

YOU'RE AN INCUMBENT OR CHALLENGER

"Everybody roots for David, nobody pulls for Goliath."

—WILT CHAMBERLAIN

REMEMBER FRIENDSTER? OR MYSPACE?

Launched in 2002, Friendster was the first online platform to allow individuals to create a personalized profile and post online content shared with friends. The predecessor to FaceMash (the original name for Facebook), Friendster invented a market and then attempted to become the dominant player. It took about two years for it to shift from inventor of an exploding market to an essentially defunct company. How did this shooting star blow up so spectacularly?

Friendster never understood that inventing a market is not the same as growing a market. They did one well and the other very poorly.

MySpace and Facebook followed Friendster into the market in 2003. Friendster quickly went from market originator and incumbent leader to also-ran by 2005, and in 2015, it mercifully closed. The reality is that it was overrun by upstart competitors in a matter of just two years. MySpace survived longer than Friendster, but never regained its short status as the leader, which it held from approximately 2004 to 2006. Facebook caught MySpace only in 2006 and has never relinquished the top spot until recently, when TikTok passed it in the global market.

Amazing how quickly the market leaders—call them "incumbents"—lose their dominant spots to companies that seem to come out of nowhere. Facebook is still a dominant incumbent, and the market now includes Instagram, Cameo, TikTok, OnlyFans, Fansly, and dozens of other players in the private-content-creation market. The reigning gorilla in the space shifted from Facebook (and Instagram, owned by Facebook) to Tik Tok and other players, which were clearly upstart challengers only a few years ago.

LIKE A NASCAR RACE

If you examine the length of time that any of these players held a dominant (or even viable) role in a crowded market, you will realize most held it only for a few short years. Much like a bumper-to-bumper NASCAR race, the leaders did not hold the lead for long, and many crashed.

For those in the scaling game, this observation underlines two key rules: 1) You must clearly recognize whether you're an incumbent or a challenger, and 2) You have fewer than five years to shift from challenger to incumbent, or you have probably missed your chance to scale.

This second rule can be badly misunderstood by companies who aspire to compete in large markets as underdogs well past their time. Chances are, the role of underdog appeals more to smaller companies, as working on a team with a "we have nothing to lose and everything to gain" attitude creates a great atmosphere. Everyone loves a great underdog victory!

As Friendster and MySpace learned the hard way, they played too long in the challenger role and never adjusted to the incumbent role. As such, aggressive competitors simply took over the market that they invented. In many ways, Friendster (and then MySpace) paid for the free "research and development" on ideas that would work, and perhaps more importantly, those that would not. All of that R & D was publicly displayed on their respective sites for competitors to either borrow liberally or avoid like the plague.

This phenomenon occurs when incumbents do not realize that they have to lead rather than simply challenge others. The role as leader is generally much harder—to compete against yourself to improve rather than to simply chase and steal market share from bigger competitors.

Friendster and MySpace mismanaged their roles in the market as incumbents and essentially paved the way for challengers to take over the market they created.

WHAT DO INCUMBENTS LOOK LIKE? CHALLENGERS?

If you and your team have been playing in your market for more than a year, you must decide how long you will play as a challenger and when you will shift from challenger to incumbent. The two roles require completely different leadership approaches and also radically different funding.

Challengers exist in a market from their founding to no longer than five years. If you enter a market, challenge the incumbents, and do not take significant market share within five years, chances are, you never will. During your incubation period of five years, the incumbent will have added further distance between you and it. You'll most likely never close that gap, and borrowing additional money to make the attempt seems irresponsible.

Check for yourself. Rewind your current market five years and notice what existed then. What did products or services look like just five years ago in your market? What pace of growth has been present for your market or industry? Have you exceeded that growth pace every year? As a challenger, you have to grow significantly faster than do the incumbents (there can be more than one) or you have zero chance of ever catching them.

Conversely, incumbents can hold that challenger position as quickly as they own a significant portion of the total market, or they can invent a tangential market niche of their own. For example, the dating app market is crowded and filled with almost any variation of customer profiles. Could you create a big enough market with a specialized niche and own it quickly? Entering into a large market with lots of players would be much preferred.

I hear this a lot: "We're entering the dating app market, because it continues to grow." The part left out: "The market is extremely crowded with incumbents who can outspend and outlast upstarts." Go find a market where you can gain traction and become a viable challenger.

As challengers, we would have to *invent* a new way to connect with available people to date, or most likely, *innovate* a market niche that no other company has figured out and attempt to own that entire niche. Notice that invention occurs when a new market is created that never before existed. Innovation (or "creativity," as most companies call it) occurs usually when a company amends or alters the already existing market.

In the dating app industry, we might innovate to create a niche for left-handed, ADHD singles. And chances are, we might face a big challenge.

In the end, consider your current situation. Which role are you playing, incumbent or challenger? Is that the correct assessment of your situation, or are you mislabeled? Is your company already past the five-year challenger expiration date, yet you still believe you can catch up to the incumbents? Is it time to shift from the leadership and attitude necessary to challenge to the leadership and attitude necessary to be a significant market player?

Once you know which role your company is playing, or rather, should be playing, you increase your chances of success in your role.

Two-Day-Old Sushi: Believing that borrowing more money (you can always find funding sources) exists as confirmation that you are (still) on the right path forward as a challenger. Like NASCAR racing teams, you can invest millions and have no wins to show for running a car and a support team. You'll only rack up larger amounts of debt. Check: Are you growing faster than your industry, while playing as a challenger? If not, you're eating two-day-old sushi.

Three-Day-Old Sushi: Confusing people-market fit with product-market fit. This trend exists when you find five to ten early adopters who love your product...and then stop. This trend can become intoxicating, as the early adopters most likely support anything you do; however, your product is only good, not good enough to steal market share. When you have a hundred or a thousand users, then you are approaching product-market fit.

The solution: Solve big problems rather than innovate or invent products. When you solve problems for customers, you create a product that customers will pay for. When you create products to show customers, some will buy the products, which might provide a false sense of security. When you then invest many months and many millions to develop the product that (only) the early adopters like, you miss the market opportunity...but still hold the debt.

Beauty Contest for Idiots: Confusing successful funding rounds with success! If you have not become viable as a company by your Series C funding (for those who like numbers, that's your third round), you most likely should reassess. Rarely does Series Dud provide better odds or better returns for the stakeholders, employees, and funding sources. Your time and market opportunity might have passed you by. If all you did was fundraise full-time, it would take you five or six years to get to Series Dud. Focus on your other responsibilities as the CEO rather than just on fundraising.

Rule #2: You must clearly recognize whether you're an incumbent or a challenger.

Rule #3: You have less than five years to shift from challenger to incumbent.

KEY LEARNING POINTS

1. You are either an incumbent player in your market, or you are a challenger to the incumbent. Know clearly which role you play!

2. If you have not built an incumbent position in five years, then you most likely never will.

3. Confusing successful fundraising with scaling does not equal succeeding and becoming a market incumbent. It generally means you have taken way too long to own a portion of your market and you exist in the gap between incumbent and challenger. It's called Series Dud for a reason.

With simple ground rules out of the way and your position in the market clearly defined, now we can turn to a subject rarely discussed: structure. A well-designed structure will scale your business much faster than culture, so let's get started.

PART 2

STRUCTURE WINS EVERY TIME

CHAPTER 3

STRUCTURE EATS CULTURE FOR BREAKFAST, LUNCH, AND DINNER

"Culture eats strategy for breakfast."

—PETER DRUCKER

In 2009, my two coaching partners and I were asked to take on a project at a large software company in the Pacific Northwest. Our job was to "bring back innovation."

Essentially, the two original founders had both departed, and the innovation thought to be baked into the company culture walked out the door with them. Our job was to rediscover and reinstall that lost innovation for its hundred thousand employees around the globe. The company's structure and products got it from inception to Fortune 50, but somewhere, its culture lost innovation in the process.

We did find the company's innovative culture and began to reinstall it...until structure bared its ferocious teeth.

A STRONG CULTURE VERSUS A BASIC STRUCTURE

Companies chirp about their great culture and compete for awards for doing so. Are you employed at one of the "Best Places to Work" in your metropolitan area or at one of the "Most Admired" companies in your sector?

Rarely do we hear about companies winning accolades for an "award-winning structure" that causes a meteoric rise. It dawned on us that when we use the word "structure" inside most companies, all at once the energy leaves the room. Consider these "sexy" structures that quietly exist in most work environments:

- Pay structure

- Legal structure

- Team structure

- Safety protocols

- Corporate structure (like an org chart)

- Compliance (government-required training and awareness)

In the case of the software company's lost innovation challenges, the answers were buried in a clash between a long-established, strong culture and a simple, rigid pay structure. Here's the simple version: the company aspired to create its highest outcomes and results in a team structure.

What's not to like? Playing on a collaborative team generally appeals to most employees. The teams did indeed produce results—just not at the pace that they had previously, when the two original founders roamed the halls. The company started buying small companies that invented useful technologies rather than simply creating the technologies in-house. This irked the CEO and COO.

The kryptonite was buried in the pay structure. The company offered generous salaries, comprehensive benefits, and stock options to all. Its employee retention was high for a software firm, mostly due to the generous salaries and benefits. In addition, tiered bonuses were earned by and paid to some *individuals*, based upon their performance and contributions to the team. The bonuses were awarded as determined by employee reviews from the team leaders. Essentially, all team members *competed* with their fellow teammates for the highest bonus, the second highest, and so on. Some members on the team got no bonuses at all.

With this simple pay structure firmly in place, you may as well toss out the strong culture surrounding "team play." The pay structure gamified and optimized a system that incentivized employees to focus mainly on earning the largest *individual* bonus, such that they could pay private school tuition and the orthodontic bill. That same pay structure forced them to compete for the largest bonus against teammates who also had private school tuition and orthodontic bills to pay. Meanwhile, the team brought in coaching and training (like my partners and me) to help them perform more seamlessly as a team, since the culture dictated that they create their highest results in teams from thirty-five to fifty people.

In theory, every person on the team liked and signed off on the idea that they could produce better results faster if they collaborated and played together. They wanted to tap the individual and collective talents of each of the members of the team, much like sports teams do. Not every player on a sports team becomes an all-star, but each can play a critical role to help win a team championship. What happens on sports teams, however, when star players sign contracts that award bonuses for all-star nominations, scoring titles, or other individual performance metrics? Often, the star players win a scoring title while their teams miss the playoffs.

Essentially, the competing agendas of the culture versus the pay structure had the organization slowly innovating, as players were reticent to share their best ideas in a team way, choosing to "ball hog" great ideas.

When the actual outcomes of the game stand in direct opposition to the stated culture, should employees share their best ideas and hope and pray that the team leader recognizes their contributions at bonus time? Perhaps a safer strategy would be to hoard their best ideas, work on them quietly in a silo, and then lobby the manager at the end of the year for the "most valuable player on the team" award. Might employees purposely avoid sharing ideas with competing "star players" on the team, since the competitors might then earn a higher bonus that they themselves might have captured?

Your kid needs braces, and so does mine. I care more about my kids (and my bank account) than I care about my colleagues, and you probably do too. The choice, then, dictated almost entirely by pay *structure*, becomes simple and obvious—hoard ideas and limit collaboration rather than share. Contribute sparingly to opposing ideas from other team members, such that my ideas might earn me the highest bonus.

Imagine the silent silos and factions that developed in the teams. We were hired to address those and assist the team to play better as one group—per the cultural mandates that everyone clearly understood. Not one person on any team ever addressed the hidden driver of the dysfunctional behavior (the need to compete against teammates for bonuses) as the root cause of the less-than-acceptable team results. As outsiders, we could spot it much more easily.

We suggested a simple remedy, used in team sports, where different players have radically different contracts and roles. The star player might earn $40M/year in salary, and a rookie might earn $500K. The other players fall somewhere in the middle of those two extremes. However, when the team wins a championship and gets a team bonus, every member of the team, even players who got injured during the season, earn an equal share bonus, since they each held one equal spot on the team. For rookies, the championship bonus share might equal their annual contracts. For the superstars, the bonus might amount to a drop in the bucket compared to their large salaries.

In the software company's disappearing innovation issue, this shared team bonus would eliminate the need to compete against teammates for orthodontics and private school tuition money. In fact, every member of the team might exceed the highest bonus awarded in the competitive bonus system, as the united team might produce far more useful results. This could drive the shared bonus pool to a much larger amount than the sum of the former individual bonuses, since the bonus pool was created for the amount of innovation and not capped. Might a collaborative team playing for one gigantic shared bonus pool produce more than fifty individuals competing against each other?

All of this hidden activity as a direct result of a pay structure negated the intended culture. It has been suggested that "culture eats strategy for breakfast." That's not entirely accurate. Structure eats culture for breakfast, lunch, dinner, and late-night snacks.

BEHAVIOR ON A SPECTRUM

In the end, any culture is malleable. Culture is also the sum of the outcomes of what we do rather than a catalyst for our behaviors. In any team with a culture, your behavior and mine is judged on a spectrum of what is acceptable rather than with a pass-fail standard. You might be highly innovative, and I, much less so. We can both play in an acceptable range on the same team and in the same organization.

In contrast, structure is fixed. Structure serves as a strong catalyst because it drives behaviors. If you disobey a safety protocol at a construction site, you are warned once and terminated the second time. There is just too much risk for you or anyone else to skirt safety practices, as coworkers could be seriously injured. This is a strong pass-fail system, or more like pass-or-get-fired system. In the case of the software company, when team members bumped up against a rigid pay structure that dictated predictable behavioral outcomes, cultural objectives began to wane rapidly and without notice.

Consider your own cultural rules, core values, or vision statement. Almost all of what is spoken and written for teams to follow exists as an ideal or a high goal. If the organization prizes innovation in its team members, then as long as you and I each demonstrate enough innovation in our tendencies, ideas, and contributions, we are safe culturally. In essence, our efforts are plotted on a spectrum of acceptable effort, perhaps more than actual contributions.

This spectrum of behavior rests as the key reason culture almost always appears as an outcome. If our team is pretty good at innovation but less proficient at another desired core value, we can change those outcomes only by incentivizing, training, or developing more of the activities we desire. As soon as the desired behaviors have to be taught or incentivized, however, we have essentially paid a tax to keep this value alive in our organization. Cultures function much better when team members *want* to move in the direction set rather than when they have to be coerced or paid to do so.

Structure, in contrast, works primarily on two far ends of the spectrum by design—fear and greed. Fear sits on one end of the spectrum, where there are clearly understood negative consequences, including termination, if we do not comply. Greed rests on the other end, where there might exist large rewards for extreme adherence, such as the individual bonuses discussed above. Play at the highest *stated* level of the structure, and you could win the biggest individual bonus...even if the contribution to the team lessens.

HIDING IN PLAIN SIGHT

Unintended consequences start to show up when senior leaders fail to notice that structure almost always wins against culture. In the case I've been discussing, the software company simply was not willing to relook at its pay structure, and the CEO eventually lost his job...not surprisingly, due to his inability to foster greater innovation. The path to shift behaviors was clear in retrospect and showed up in the form of a perverse bonus structure. Innovation could only flourish when all talents collaborated for best results. The team members knew what the CEO would not acknowledge—that the pay structure was gamified by the team members for individual advantages.

Structure serves as one catalyst that alters culture—never the other way around. Companies spend an inordinate amount of time and energy building a healthy and productive culture, often without realizing that culture always shows up as the *outcome* of what activities actually take place rather than the catalyst that drives those behaviors.

Structure is rigid and strong, on purpose. Culture is the ultimate game of "soft" skills—namely, how we treat each other as we work and play together. Soft rarely pushes around rigid, even though we might like to think that to be true. In the softer game, our actions, words, and contributions are much more nuanced. In our structural activities, we have either adhered to the safety protocols and successfully completed the sexual harassment education, or we are put on notice. No one has ever "competed" for the prize of Valedictorian of the sexual harassment course mandated by federal law. You comply, or you do not comply. Hence, the outcomes in terms of behavior are much more predictable.

A simple example might prove the point. If your culture is built on respecting and partnering with your coworkers, then can you simply cancel sexual harassment training, since a respectful culture would prevent incidents of sexual harassment?

Culture is the result or outcome of how the organization reacts and behaves when a complaint or lawsuit is levied against the company. Culture never acts as the catalyst to prevent the suit from occurring in the first place. If it did, sexual harassment awareness training would prevent most incidents. It does not, as the number of sexual harassment lawsuits has exploded rather than declined.

If you're not so sure about the power of structure in your organization, just ask for an exception from the legal department on your participation and adherence to sexual harassment policies. See if your corporate lawyers are willing to waive the requirement for you, given your high respect for others.

Problem is, most companies do not build their teams at all on structure, but primarily on culture instead...which is ironic, since structure actually drives behaviors, and culture is the end result of how the organization behaves.

KEY LEARNING POINTS

1. Structure and culture are both omnipresent in your organization. They hold very different roles in your team.

2. Structure drives activities—wanted and unwanted. Culture encourages desired outcomes.

3. Structure tends to be very rigid, and as such, generally wins against cultural initiatives that differ.

Your first task in setting up your business to scale is to build all structures with a direct connection to succeeding at your commercial vision.

Next up, we'll explore some powerful structural practices that help companies scale and introduce the first exponential practice.

CHAPTER 4

THERE'S ONLY ONE MISSION IN THE SCALING GAME

"What I've learned is the power of a compelling vision."

—ALAN MULALLY

MEET DAVID SIEGEL, CEO OF MEETUP, THE WILDLY POPULAR connection and events platform. For twenty years, fifty million people have chosen Meetup to make real connections over the things that matter to them.

David became CEO a year before the pandemic and inherited an organization that loved to connect people in active settings, *in person* rather than online. In fact, for the first eighteen years of the company's existence, a user could be banned from the Meetup community for creating and hosting a group that met exclusively online. Meetup always viewed its platform only one way: *use technology to get people off technology!*

Its culture and mission were pretty clear. Meetup had a mission that scaled in direct proportion to the rise in phone and laptop use. As people became more digitally (over)connected, Meetup groups organized and hosted wine tastings, hikes, sports clubs—almost anything that involved people enjoying activities in person. This simple idea brought people together and grew quickly. Meetup served a high purpose by fulfilling its commercial vision of growing its business.

Then came the pandemic.

The news came slowly at first, and with it, increasing fear. Then on March 10, 2020, the country essentially locked down. Working at most business buildings ceased, all retail shops closed, and, with no timetable given for a reprieve, people remained nervously at home. No more friends over for dinner. No YMCA league basketball. No movie theaters. No restaurant dining.

David had been a successful CEO before, running both Investopedia and Seeking Alpha, before taking the lead role at Meetup in 2019. He understood the role of a new CEO who replaces the founder.

In his own words: "When you come in as a new CEO, one of two strategies need to take place. You look at the current model and change or expand revenue channels, which was the case at Investopedia. Alternatively, you can simplify and decide to focus on fewer revenue opportunities and capture them better, which was the preferred strategy at Meetup."

David was thriving in his new role, with a team that enjoyed their work and impact on people. Meetup succeeded well financially when members got off their phones and enjoyed time with people at an event that mattered to participants. Meetup's team had one job: provide an easy-to-use platform and tools to host successful in-person events.

On March 10, David had an immediate decision to make. He needed to reconsider the commercial mission of the business. After all, there really is only one mission when scaling, and it's commercial!

Here's how you know.

Had David and his team continued banning members who hosted online events, they would have dropped revenue to near zero and most likely folded, waiting futilely for a stubborn pandemic to ease. The tradition that had worked until then would have mandated the banning of members, at a time when in-person events simply disappeared.

Would the investors (Meetup was owned by WeWork, prior to its sale to AlleyCorp), employees, or members have cared about a historically cultural precedent, only to watch the entire organization fold? Had there been a venture capital firm involved, would it have given David high praise for "sticking to his guns" and keeping with the initial idea of using technology to get people off technology, all while the company failed?

Sticking to the historical precedent most likely would have gotten David fired over time. After all, a cultural vision with no promise for commercial success equals a pipe dream. It also cancels any cultural vision at the same time. And if you don't have a company, you also don't have a culture.

Instead, David met with his team and announced that Meetup would immediately shift its entire platform and not only create virtual groups, but also partner with members to host successful *online* events. By Friday, March 15, just five days after a worldwide lockdown, Meetup had redefined its mission to be more in line with connecting people rather than *how* they connected.

Long-time employees had a difficult time with the change. Online events went against everything the company had ever stood for. Without any idea of how long the lockdown would last, might the organization just "wait and see" before abandoning a founding tenet of the company?

David did not flinch. He knew that a commercially viable mission was the only key to keeping the mission and vision of the company. Ironically, David realized that the quick shift simply accelerated what would have happened naturally in the coming five to seven years. The pandemic just forced the issue. He led the rapid change.

Two years since this shift, the most frequent question from Meetup organizers is whether online events will persist after the pandemic. And the answer is yes. The company has heard countless stories of yoga groups, dance groups, and others who had only a dozen members at events pre-pandemic who now often have double or triple that number since the potential audience is a global audience. Any of Meetup's 56 million members can now access and attend any event throughout the entire world and meet people who are even more different from them. The pivot was a success.

David was not so connected to the historical vehemence against online events, so he was in a better position to reconsider Meetup's actual mission: to connect people. The method and platform made much less difference than did addressing the human need for connection, and a pandemic offered the perfect opportunity to reconsider the manner in which the team would assist members in doing just that.

In the end, the Meetup platform has hosted over five million online events, and over thirty million members have attended an online event—from virtually zero in its first eighteen years! For many people completely stuck at home, the online events served a vital purpose of connecting when connection was limited. They served as a true life source that made isolation far more bearable for millions.

David fulfilled the only mission any scaling company has to achieve—the commercial mission. In doing so, Meetup actually expanded its cultural mission, as the platform now holds two different robust markets (in-person and online events), significantly expanding its impact.

Now say hello to Tom Szaky, founder and CEO of TerraCycle, a company with a simple mission "to eliminate the idea of waste." Created while Tom was at Princeton as an undergrad, the company has grown exponentially and emerged as the leader of not just unconventional recycling efforts across the globe, but even more importantly, of the idea that waste need not exist. As an example, TerraCycle recycles used disposable diapers. If it takes the mission far enough, could it recycle spent uranium rods from power plants?

Why not?

Tom and his team have scaled in large part because the company's market continues to grow, and since much waste is not profitable to recycle or reuse, Tom and his team need to invent ways to achieve the mission and do so at a profit.

Important to note is that TerraCycle is a "for-profit" company, looking to make money as much as any other. If it issues an IPO, investors will have a voice in continuing that march to further profitability. So how, then, does Tom weigh the competing agendas of recycling materials that cannot yet be recycled profitably and keeping stakeholders happy with financial results?

In Tom's own words: "When raising large amounts of capital, I could frame the capital raise in terms of the valuation of the company. If I did that, I would most likely lose team members internally, because that does not reinforce our purpose. Instead, I have to frame our capital raise in terms of the impact, or the additional amount of good we could do. Similarly, I frame our profitability and cash on hand as the key to our being able to do our work for a sustained length of time rather than our price per share.

"In the early years, we actually had people send us money as a donation, because they saw we did the work that non-profits normally did. We found that it was much easier to project purpose when we were small and broke. As we have become more financially robust, we simply have to be very cognizant to put the mission out front rather than lifestyle or corporate excesses. If we signed up for a posh office, we would immediately be seen as hypocritical, as our success should multiply our ability to eliminate the idea of waste rather than create reserved parking stalls for our leadership team's new Italian sports cars. That would just never happen."

Does this mean that Tom simply raises capital to subsidize really unprofitable waste items? Here's Tom again: "Consider the idea of acquiring another company, which we see as a viable way to do more. I would much rather acquire a company with healthy financials and balance sheet and enroll them in (more) purpose, than the other way around. It's just too challenging to change the business fundamentals of an organization. In the end, we can do more good with robust financials.

"The two places where a very high purpose really helps is in fundraising, as the interest is very high in the investment community for profitable companies who do good in the world. Secondly, we can recruit high-level talent much more efficiently, because many people would rather invest their talents in our company's mission than for a company solely looking to raise their share price.

"We are also clear that we will partner with almost any company, even if they get some goodwill for partnering with us to clean up the mess that they helped create."

Case in point, TerraCycle partners with big oil and big tobacco. Tom avoids the moral stand and simply focuses on recycling used cigarette butts. Tom does not condemn customers, but rather partners with them to recycle. The credit for cleaning up the mess is shared, and the customer is almost better known than TerraCycle. This holds true for cigarette companies, fast food chains, and cosmetic brands.

In the end, Tom Szaky and David Siegel understand fully that the mission to fulfill is clear: achieve your commercial mission as the most effective path to scaling.

WHAT ABOUT YOUR MISSION?

If you're going to scale, your commercial mission takes precedence over any sort of cultural vision. Like Meetup and TerraCycle, the commercial mission provides the gateway to achieving anything cultural, and failing commercially wrecks any shot at your cultural vision.

Look at your own company mission. Is it direct? Does it solve a big problem or create something new?

If not, chances are your mission to scale lives in cultural form only. That's great as long as you are ready to look your parents in the eye and tell them the story of how you lost their retirement funds...because your commercial mission was never fulfilled.

Your first task in setting up your business to scale: develop a simple, compelling *commercial* vision.

KEY LEARNING POINTS

1. Your company holds only one mission, and it's commercial.

2. Your commercial mission creates a direct, tangible path to what you want to accomplish in your market or in the world.

3. Without a commercial mission, your cultural mission does not exist.

4. No stakeholder or investor will ever congratulate you for creating an award-winning culture if, at the same time, you are failing in your commercial venture.

With your vision in place, now it's time to consider the idea of working with or without a chip on your shoulder. Which chip works most effectively for your team, including no chip at all?

SCALING PRACTICE #1:
CREATING A COMPELLING COMMERCIAL VISION

As suggested, a compelling cultural vision that scales plus a commercial vision that fails equals a failure of both. Here are simple steps to developing your vision for scaling—your commercial mission:

Step #1: Focus on developing and articulating your commercial vision solely rather than confusing (or promoting) two visions—cultural versus commercial.

Step #2: Avoid jargon such as "best in class," "industry leading," and "exceeding expectations." These are very hard to quantify, prove, or defend.

Step #3: Avoid slogans, catch phrases, or bumper stickers.

As an example, when David Siegel took over Meetup, the company used: *Meetups for everyone, everywhere.* As David suggested, "It provided absolutely no focus." He shifted it (with team input) to: *Empowering personal growth through real human connections.*

Step #4: Use simple language.

Step #5: Use one sentence only. No manifestos or sermons.

Consider JFK's mission for NASA in 1961: "*I believe that this nation should commit itself to achieving the goal, before this decade is out, of landing a man on the moon and returning him safely to the earth.*"

Step #6: Clearly state the condition for satisfaction. Consider Tom Szaky and TerraCycle's commercial vision: *Eliminate the idea of waste.*

Step #7: Provide a direct path from inception to success, without the details of the journey. For example, SpaceX might simply say: *Our vision is to successfully colonize Mars.*

CHAPTER 5

DOES A CHIP ON YOUR SHOULDER SCALE BETTER THAN NONE?

"Great players always play with a chip on their shoulder no matter if they have a reason to or not."

—CHRISTIAN MCCAFFREY

DO YOU EVER GET REALLY WORKED UP ABOUT SOMETHING just to prove you're right? It could be finally beating your older sibling at a game of Scrabble or tennis, or it could be justifying someone's support (or doubt) in you.

It's called "playing with a chip on your shoulder," and at one time in your life, you probably did so. In its best form, a chip dramatically focuses your attention, drives your actions, and allows you to endure more significant challenges and hardships than had you worked without a chip.

I was married at eighteen, and my first daughter was born after my first semester of college. I was the fourth of nine kids, and my parents were understandably not pleased with my choices. My mom declared that I would never succeed, since I would now have to forego a higher education (a very clear expectation in our family) in lieu of working menial jobs to support my young family. In essence, I would drop from the ranks of the college-educated to do "blue collar" work. That was a complete moral failure in our home, since our parents sacrificed to put all of us through private, college-preparatory high schools.

My own kids will tell you most members of our family are genetically predisposed to have a "stubborn and unreasonable" gene, and I most likely got a double dose, one from each parent. In its positive form, stubbornness shows up like sheer will and determination to finish an unreasonable task—like graduating from college in four years while holding down two full-time jobs.

At the time, I was simply bound and determined to prove my mom wrong, and that pursuit almost killed me; I worked both the swing shift and the graveyard shift for four years, all while taking a full load of classes to stay on track for a four-year degree. In the end, I rarely went to classes (in lieu of naps), but instead used the graveyard shift (as a security guard) to figure out the coursework on my own. It wasn't a typical college experience, but it worked to get me from semester to semester in a prestigious university.

I was simply unwilling to take longer than four years to graduate because, if I did, I would allow my mom to be right. Did I mention I'm stubborn and unreasonable? I did graduate, on time, second-from-the-bottom of my class, with a three-year-old daughter and wife by my side, in what really was a family effort.

All of this due to a severe chip on my shoulder.

In interviews with successfully scaling companies, I learned that most CEOs clearly identify with the power of working with a chip on the shoulder for their organizations. There is clearly no "one size fits all," as some chips described were negative or almost angry in nature, and some were more aspirationally centered. Chips were internally and externally facing, and the one unifying tenet continued to appear: working with a chip on your shoulder facilitates greater focus and unity from the organization and can optimize or improve performance.

Some might argue that this is essentially a cultural tool and, as such, should be optional. But consider this: since the lowest-performance group in my research contained companies with no chips at all, why would you not deploy the full power of this practice in a structural move to unite around an agreed-upon cause?

But only if you deploy the most useful chip...

THREE TYPES OF CHIPS

"The bully on the playground" (externally facing chip)

By far, most companies deploy this chip, with good reason. It is the easiest to deploy, and in agreeing upon a common enemy, the team rallies around fighting against a perceived or real bully figure. Usually, this bully appears in the form of a close competitor, a dominant market force (like Amazon), or an oppressive governing body of some kind (like the FDA). The bully could even appear in the form of an unsolved or "unsolvable" challenge.

Regardless, once the team has agreed upon the bully and gotten progressively worked up about it, focus becomes much easier to garner, as everyone wants to take out the bully, and the gamification process naturally follows—with no violence, just shared attention and energy toward winning.

Ring a bell every time a new customer signs up as a result of your team stealing the customer from the bully! Enjoy a team lunch every time you steal more than a prescribed number of new customers in a month. Earn gift cards when you close on a new customer taken directly from the bully. You get the idea.

The focus becomes clear. Strategies and tactics follow quickly, and results begin to appear. The bully rarely knows nor cares that it plays a useful role. Mostly, it provides a target to unite your team!

Say hello to Aaron Phillips, CEO of SitePro, a software company that provides real-time access to fluid management data across even the most complex system of tanks, pipelines, and trucks in the oil exploration field.

Oil exploration, drilling, and management of oil production all have one thing in common: they are not for the faint-hearted. Since the first oil tycoons, the oil business has consisted of a treacherous playing field where you have to take risks, from managing a market price for crude (which you cannot control) to selecting potential drilling spots that may or may not pay off. You must be willing to accept all the risks, or you should clearly play in another industry.

The players are tough, the competition tougher, so I asked Aaron if he plays with a chip on his shoulder, as if he has something to prove.

"Of course!" came his simple reply.

You see, Aaron was pursuing an advanced degree, on the brink of failure, when one mathematics professor turned on the proverbial light. "All of a sudden, Calculus 3 made total sense, even though I did not really understand much calculus up to that point."

With this newfound clarity and understanding, Aaron went on to write a dissertation that led to his PhD, soon realizing that publishing a thesis makes all of the contents part of the public domain. In short, anyone could utilize his proprietary ideas, without thanking Aaron or paying him for it. Aaron got some credit, but no cash.

"I did all the work. I wrote up the findings, and suddenly, after a presentation or talk somewhere, other people were using my proprietary intellectual property to make money. I got zero!"

Aaron did a quick pivot and patented his ideas instead from that point forward. He walked away from the entire PhD process, six months before finishing. "You bet I had a chip on my shoulder! I was going to show these guys what I could do, especially since I understood the technology better than any of them. I was going to beat them in the field!"

That patented technology allows customers full visibility into their entire operations. This full visibility allows customers to see areas that need attending to before issues occur. Aaron's proprietary software, once given away for free, now acts as the cornerstone of his entire company.

Aaron's experience, although perhaps more dramatic than most, highlights a simple idea. When you have something to prove, you play differently. Better? Harder? More focused? Perhaps even angrier?

Check all of the above that apply to you.

This idea proved to be true in every industry and in every company size. Inventing a common enemy, whether it be a competitor you want to take deals from or a large goal with big challenges you want to chase, the chip helped in multiple ways and was connected to higher growth than companies that had no chips.

How much higher?

Compared to no chip whatsoever, a unified focus on an external adversary or attitude drives scale 7.3% faster, or raises revenue year over year by that same amount. Ironically, companies with no chip have nothing to compare to, since they do not deploy the idea. CEO after CEO suggested that inventing a common enemy was one of the first things they did upon taking the job. It simply unites all players, focuses attention on the desired outcome, and helps to scale faster than working without a chip.

Taking on this *externally facing chip on the shoulder* makes lots of sense and seems pretty simple both to identify and implement. If the eight-hundred-pound gorilla controls your market, your objective might be super clear: take (read: steal) 100 customers, $100K, or 100 employees from that competitor. Every time you do, your team gains more confidence, and you feel like you are winning!

"Is that the best we can do?" (internally facing chip)

Well, if there exists an externally facing chip on the shoulder, how might that compare to an *internally* facing chip? More importantly, might the latter type of chip help you to scale even faster?

Meet Lisa Alderson, the Founder and CEO of Genome Medical, a telehealth medical practice. Lisa leads a team that provides expert genetic healthcare for individuals and their families to improve health and well-being.

Genome Medical is Lisa's seventh start-up, and her sense is that a rallying cry works to get the right people around the company table. In Lisa's own words: "I find that a mission-driven rallying cry attracts the right people and purposely repels those who are not the right fit. We connect around our mission in a way that unites us in one purpose.

"I have found that meaningful work combined with an incredible team is an even stronger magnet for talent than financial incentives alone. Stock options and bonuses are great but they can provide undesired focus on the wrong type of growth if you're not careful. For an employer who attracts talent solely due to compensation, it's easy to see attrition if a higher-paying package comes along. That's not how I like to build a team. I want every member of the team to be fully connected to our purpose. Otherwise, they may simply go elsewhere for more money. We focus less on competition and more on how we work with each other and how we bring the talents of our organization together to achieve our desired outcomes. We simply play to get better as an organization day after day, month after month."

Like Lisa and her team, try the internally focused chip for yourself.

Imagine that you finally break the eight-minute mile pace for running a 10K. You don't then set your target on beating Olympic runners who run the same race at half that pace, do you? That's a bit like thinking that your one-hundred-person company is going to overthrow Google or Amazon as its next goal. The focus would fall flat very quickly.

Rather than focusing attention on a common enemy, being externally focused, much like an athlete is, the more useful chip might be one focused on internally focused improvements. This amounts to focusing on lowering your average mile time from eight minutes down to 7:45. Such a goal is not only achievable, but it unleashes all types of benefits while you are in the process of succeeding. The internally focused chip on the shoulder is tied to increases in self-confidence (multiplied by the number of people on any given team), learning, growth, and increased ambition. The compounding effect of each of these benefits makes the internally focused chip extremely effective...for the right organization.

Much like a good 10K runner working toward the leap it takes to compete in a half marathon, you can use an internally focused chip on the shoulder to optimize and focus on micro-steps and goals, such that the team can incrementally take on the needed improvements toward scale. At times, the pace of improvements might feel overly ambitious, and in the end, the scaling of talents creates the commercial gains. Most companies keep some sort of financial scorecard, and we've found that the month-over-month compounded effect of continual improvement—demonstrated in the form of challenging your-self to become better than you were just one month earlier—scales almost twice as effectively as an externally focused chip.

But it's not for everyone.

This internally focused chip on the shoulder has proven to be less popular; after all, we always focus on others first when we need to blame someone! Yet it is more effective for scaling than an externally focused chip—13.8% better (or faster). The reason boils down to the increased focus on exactly what is needed to improve inside an organization, compared with wasting a portion of resources to chase a competitor or objective. After all, chasing Amazon is not a bad idea, but it will invariably lead you to places in which you cannot compete. That's suboptimal at best, even if you do take some of Amazon's business.

In Lisa's case, Genome Medical's growth rate has proven the real prize for creating an internal chip in the form of a rallying cry. "We have been really pleased with our growth to date, and I attribute that to each member of our team committing to both our mission and their individual part in improving every day!"

Beauty Contest for Idiots: Choosing a chip based upon circumstances that simply do not exist. For the vast major-ity of companies, an externally focused chip is the most appropriate and quickest to deploy. But pretending you are a different company than actually exists creates an ineffective chip and could backfire. For example, most companies start with a solution to a problem that another company has failed to address well. Your chip would most likely be best suited to "go after" taking business from this company as proof that you are succeeding rather than setting an internal goal of competing against yourself each month.

One is more appropriate, given your stage and size. At best, your results will most likely not mirror the growth rates shown.

A third kind of chip? How about internally focused with a global impact?

Remember Tom Szaky, CEO of TerraCycle, from the last chapter? His global recycling company is eliminating the idea of waste. Although it is a commercial venture, people still send donations to the firm. TerraCycle proves that doing good things can and does pay handsomely.

But does TerraCycle scale better than a typical for-profit company?

I asked Tom if he thought having a chip on his shoulder helped his bid to scale, which the company has done extremely well. We had early data that supported a chip as a more effective way to focus attention and the idea that creating a common rival or enemy (usually a big competitor) unites the team.

Tom agreed, and then let us in on his secret.

"Throughout our history (founded in a dorm room at Princeton in 2002), we have fought to hire top talent, but with this limitation: TerraCycle could not pay what much larger companies could. I could find great talent, but then had to convince candidates to work at a far lower wage scale than they could earn elsewhere, sometimes as much as one-fifth the market rate.

"We recognized that we appealed well to two demographics: the younger, idealistic, first-job-out-of-school people, and the last-job-I'll-ever-have people."

The young, idealistic category is clear to understand. The last-job category seems less clear. Tom explained that if you are essentially done with writing big checks for your kids' educations, mortgages, and weddings, and you are toiling away at a role that is unfulfilling, the prospect of working your final ten years in an industry or cause you believe in makes far more sense than "chasing the money." Tom looks for these types of unfulfilled, very talented people for his leadership team, as TerraCycle provides the platform such that they never have to work another day in an industry for which they might need to apologize. Their work addresses a huge problem and makes progress in solving it!

Recycling everything—from used disposable diapers to clothing to used motor oil—appeals to lots of people. Most never act on their ethics and desire to make a difference, because they are too distracted by other things, like making money and furthering their career ambitions. Tom realizes that the last-job folks' wisdom and talent are at the highest points of their careers. He need only invite them to invest that great talent in a great cause.

For those who do choose to make a difference in a company they believe in, TerraCycle creates the most effective type of chip on the shoulder—the internally facing pursuit of an impact or purpose-driven objective rather than the pursuit of a profit or stock price. This pursuit is traditionally found only in non-profit causes, but Tom and his team are interested in creating a profit, and their main purpose for doing so is tied directly and proportionally to the amount of progress they make in recycling literally anything.

"Ironically, not focusing primarily on financial gain and challenging ourselves to get better each month actually provides growth that is higher than externally focused metrics, like a stock price. Our chip drives internally, impact-measured metrics and drives profit. We chase the increased impact for the good of the planet, and that drives profitability. The combination creates a rich platform where our team never has to consider whether people are calling in sick, because they want to pursue their cause every single day. If they are sick, they call in, but never with the "phantom flu."

Difficult to find, companies and causes such as TerraCycle "compete" only against themselves (using an internally facing chip). They have to invent their own ambitions, since the challenges facing them daily will always dwarf their ability to fully solve them. Their jobs never end, and those who play on the team earn the daily satisfaction that the challenging work they do makes a lasting, positive effect—again, a compounding effect created by an internally motivated desire to improve.

This internally focused, purpose platform generates the fastest scaling model found.

A WORD TO THE WISE

Two-Day-Old Sushi: It's tempting to go for the highest return on the chip and create an internal, purpose-driven platform akin to TerraCycle. But inventing your "why" and using it as the purpose that will drive scale does not equate to actually having a purpose that makes a gigantic impact in the real world. In the end, your "why" is just that—your own. The rest of the world most likely cares little about it, as it affects only you.

Choose the chip on your shoulder that drives growth. For most companies, that starts with an external focus. Eventually, shifting to an internal chip improves the results, but the key remains the same: customize your chip for the best results rather than the best bragging rights. The world will care a whole lot more about robust financial results than they care about your chosen chip.

KEY LEARNING POINTS

1. A chip on your shoulder drives scale better than none at all.

2. There exist three kinds of chips: 1) externally facing, 2) internally focused, and 3) internally focused with a global impact.

3. Deploy the chip that represents where your company exists. It will provide the most benefit.

With your commercial vision clear and a boost in drive from employing the most appropriate chip on your shoulder, now let's consider the most powerful tool we uncovered in our CEO interviews. It's called One Core Directive, and it's time to play.

SCALING PRACTICE #2:
DEPLOYING A CHIP ON YOUR SHOULDER

There exists two categories of chips to deploy: 1) externally facing and 2) internally focused. A rare third type, internally focused with a global impact, should be considered only with very specific criteria in place.

To create your own chip, consider the following:

Step #1: Decide if the proposed chip will unite focus and camaraderie. If not, restate it in such a way that everyone jumps on board. (Note: Avoid sports' analogies when creating a chip as that alienates some members of the team.)

Step #2: Most importantly, choose the type of chip that best suits where you are in your company maturation. Internally focused chips work much better with teams who know and trust each other more. If you are not at that stage, deploy the externally facing chip as the most effective choice, and then consider changing later.

For externally facing chips:

Step #1: Pick a reasonable number or metric for your team to "win" against the competitor. There's no reason to attempt to take something from a competitor that is far too ambitious, will fall way short, and then will dampen team morale. Much better to pick an initial target that seems reasonable, and adjust the target moving forward.

Step #2: Gamify the objective. That could involve symbolic prizes, team lunches, high fives—almost anything. The team has to enjoy going after an external competitor, or they will not play.

Step #3: Make the chip about something other than just sales goals. This will make sure that everyone gets to play as well as celebrate the wins.

For internally focused chips:

Step #1: Set your baseline target from last month. Let's say you got eight new contracts installed. That becomes your baseline.

Step #2: Now ask the team this simple question: "What would it take to hit eleven contracts next month?" You are not doubling sales. You are looking for a new personal best. Rinse and repeat for months, until the game stalls out.

Step #3: Consider changing metrics or outcomes, such that the game does not get stale. Some outcomes are useful for years. Others peter out much more quickly. Change your chip as necessary.

CHAPTER 6

THE SIMPLEST TOOL TO SCALE YOUR BUSINESS

"That's been one of my mantras—focus and simplicity. Simple can be harder than complex: You have to work hard to get your thinking clean and make it simple. But it's worth it in the end because once you get there, you can move mountains."

—STEVE JOBS

AN ASTONISHINGLY HIGH PERCENTAGE OF COMPANIES LIST their core values—the supposed foundation of the culture that should empower great talent and inclusion—in multiple linguistic forms; for example, single values (like integrity, creativity, or fairness) mixed with full sentences, with metaphors thrown in for good measure. This mix of linguistic styles rarely clarifies, and in times of crisis, actually confuses people.

Might the failure rate (9 in 10) for new companies follow a similar percentage of companies using these confusing linguistic formats?

Here's the two-day-old sushi form of core values, copied by most companies—as if a 10% success rate is worthy of copying.

1. **Individual one-word attributes,** *often followed by a short definition.* Honesty is a great example, as is creativity, loyalty, empathy, service—the list goes on. Regardless of the intended power of your one-word core value, if you have to explain exactly what you mean, doesn't that indicate that we are all at risk to misinterpret or misapply the value?

2. **Statements of belief.** For example, "We love our customers!" Do we? Always? Really? What happens when we don't? Do we disengage with customers unilaterally, or do we fire clients who do not reciprocate our loving feelings? What about chronically "unlovable" clients? Is our belief statement (one of the pillars of the company value system) operational without the shared love of both parties?

3. **Metaphors or cliches.** "Play chess, not checkers!" What do you tell team members who have never played one or both games? Given the increasing diversity of many organizations, what if your teammate learned Go instead of chess? What

if you play Sudoku, a very different game than checkers or chess? Metaphors stand at great risk of being misunderstood. Chess, checkers, Go, or Sudoku are best left for the breakroom, not the foundational beliefs of the company.

4. *A mix of all three.* Many companies engage in multiple formats—mixing and matching individual one-word attributes with statements of belief and, finally, metaphors. Your team ends up with a blended, confusing mess. Most values then get combined with a long explanation of what is meant, every additional word further diluting their usefulness.

5. *Copying attractive-sounding values from a successful company...that are clearly not yours!* How many companies do you know that have borrowed "debate and decide" because Amazon uses it? It's a bit like borrowing a set of clothes from a star athlete. The jersey might look good, but your athletic talent does not improve by wearing it.

SHIFTING BEHAVIOR. HOW WE REALLY DECIDE.

When you bought your last car, how much research did you do prior to purchase? If you're like most, you answered something like, "I looked at the Honda Accord, the Ford Fusion Hybrid, and the Toyota Camry."

Your research most likely compared price, gas mileage or EV range, warranties, and quality ratings. Eventually, you bought a car.

But where did the *initial* list of cars come from? Why was the comparable Hyundai, Acura, Chevy, and Audi model not on your list?

The amount of data we avoid far outweighs the data we actually engage. In reality, we form most decisions by what we *think, feel, believe, or remember*. We then find data to *confirm* our decision. To us, it sounds like research. To others, it tends to sound like justification.

With cars, the quality of most models is high enough that your research could confirm almost any brand or model you like. Did you dismiss Audis because you *believe* they are really expensive to service? Depending upon how you assess the cost of maintenance, Audis perform very well in the (low) cost maintenance category, as they require maintenance far less often over time. When you do finally get a tune-up, it does cost more than other brands, but it needs maintenance less frequently.

For Hyundais, did you *feel* like their quality is not as good as the other brands? When pushed, consumers assessed Hyundai as a "low-quality" car brand, since their price is lower. Price and quality are completely separate, but we can easily convince ourselves that lower price must equate to lower quality.

Our car example affects mostly us, but what if we follow the same premise for the building and scaling of a company culture? Might our beliefs start to impact our chances of scaling?

When Airbnb first started, an almost universal belief was that you should never allow strangers into your home, even if they paid you for the privilege. Wouldn't those renters rifle through your underwear drawer?

EVERYONE believed this premise, until the three founders showed that belief to be unfounded. Within two years, their dismissal of this belief manifested itself in two rules for Airbnb hosts and guests:

- Be a good host.

- Be a good house guest.

Notice they did not have one-word values, statements of belief, or metaphors. With two simple directives (two sides of the same coin, if you will), they preemptively solved most issues between landlords and renters.

As the company matured, renters started to stray from this simple set of values. Guests threw parties against the landlords' wishes. Trouble ensued. Viral videos and neighbor complaints began. All because simple directives were ignored.

If you rent from an Airbnb host, do you leave a great review? A good house guest certainly would, if the place was delivered as advertised.

If you are a host, do you provide a list of the best coffee shops, restaurants, and local attractions? Do you leave the Wi-Fi code in many locations, such that guests can access it easily?

Considerate guests and hosts do these simple things, and a billion-dollar industry was birthed. Scaling would not have happened as quickly if the Airbnb founders copied the core values of another unicorn.

BEAUTY CONTEST FOR IDIOTS

Bumper stickers declare, "My grandchild is cuter than your grandchild." Fair enough for proud grandparents. Why pick that fight with an older lady who might knock you out? Funny, though, no one ever wears a "World's Worst Dad" shirt, though technically the worst dad must exist if there also exists a greatest dad. Which dad would fall directly on the median line? Should we offer all dads percentile ranks, such that dads everywhere can compete for their effective rankings and post them on their LinkedIn bios?

CEOs and founders are no different than proud grandparents. They think their culture is better than ours...and most CEOs dramatically overrate ugly babies!

Winning this game is akin to entering and winning a beauty contest for idiots! If a higher percentage of companies fail than succeed, then your culture stands a decent chance of failure. Why then chirp about how great your culture is, or at least not until after you have succeeded commercially?

When asked where and when the core values of most companies were developed, CEOs and founders offer up some version of the early offsite story, where they "figured them all out" with the early team. Typically, they propose many. They debate. They whittle down the number at some point. Eventually, the team who began at the early offsite comes away with an "awesome" set of values as the foundation of the company culture!

Like shopping for a car, where did the initial candidates come from, and why were other options never considered?

THE POP QUIZ YOU NEED TO TAKE

I typically inquire about the embryonic fluid of any company—in short, the values instituted since the beginning—that still direct behavior years later. Try this short pop quiz to know if it's time to revisit the core values your company holds in your embryonic fluid:

- Can you state the core values of your company, in the order that they exist on your website?

- Do you need to explain what you mean by any of your core values?

- Do you have three, five, seven, or even more core values?

- Is the linguistic structure (single words, statements of belief, or metaphors) consistent in all of your values, or do you mix and match styles?

When starting out, the Airbnb founders solved the two main concerns held by the landlords and the renters—essentially, treat your counterparts like you would like to be treated. They spoke both as directives, not suggestions. The suggestions seemed like common sense, and they were created for the right kind of landlord and the right kind of house guest.

The founders knew exactly why they chose those values. They anticipated that the two chosen values would proactively solve most problems and would make it clear who to ban from their platform and who to allow to remain. If you were an inconsiderate host or house guest, they took no chances with you. Not following a simple code risked the success of the entire platform!

They could solve many problems with two simple directives, and they did not need a committee to review offenses. Almost anyone in the organization could handle a guest who threw a party, caused damages, and received a police report, as the solution is obvious.

At your initial offsite, chances are that very late nights were in play...as might have been alcohol and other substances! What was probably not in attendance was any threat or immediate challenge to the proposed cultural values. In an offsite, planning tends to focus on blue skies and clear sailing, especially when designing a culture. We design for a big success, rarely for our worst nightmare.

One giant blind spot shows up only when the culture creators figure out that hundreds and even thousands of companies with essentially the same values spoken in the same hierarchical order, even in the same industry, have failed miserably. If culture were really the most important lever to scale a company, why then would you pick a set of values that has repeatedly failed others?

Here are some blind spots that constitute a beauty contest for idiots. Picking cultural values based upon the leadership team or solely by the founders often occurs in a bit of a vacuum that includes these major limitations:

1. The cultural values are positive in nature (terrific!) and built only for your best days, not for when you are struggling or in crisis mode. Essentially, this blind spot equates to a camping trip with no tents and very little food, because "no rain is in the forecast this weekend, and we're going to catch a ton of fish for dinner."

2. The cultural values are completely disconnected from the commercial objective. For example,

creativity is a commonly held, highly-prized value. That's great for many firms, but what if you run an assembly plant, where execution, efficiency, and precision might improve your chances for success? How about a nuclear power plant? Does creativity play well in an arena with major safety and compliance regulations?

A CEO recently glowed in his interview about his company's #1 core value: *kindness*. I loved the value, but I asked him if he could offer a direct path from this core value to commercial success, since he wants to build a large company. He struggled for a moment, as no one had ever asked him to do this. He pushed back at the question, saying kindness was a scaling lever because working in an atmosphere where people are treated kindly empowers an improved workplace. I readily agreed. How, though, did it help everyone to succeed in the commercial venture?

He realized that he had designed a cultural foundation that works primarily when things are mostly going well.

When asked what happened the last time a team member fell way short of expectations, made a big mistake, or put the company's future at risk, the CEO retold a recent example. He recalled when the marketing lead took on an assignment in which he had three weeks to prepare a slide presentation suitable for a key sales meeting. The prospective customer being presented to would provide the first significant revenue for the company and effectively launch them as real players in their market.

On the day of the presentation, shortly before the meeting, the marketing lead suggested that another week would be needed, or else the company might be poorly represented. In short, after three weeks with no warnings, he offered a postponement with almost no notice! Embarrassing for the team. Embarrassing for the CEO. With a real risk of losing the prospect.

I asked how kindness entered into the debrief conversation with this team member—a leader in the organization. The CEO took great pains to say that he gave straight-forward feedback, much of it negative, and reminded the marketing lead that he could have jeopardized a very large revenue source. He did so, however, with "as much kindness as possible." When I asked what the CEO was actually feeling during the conversation, he finally admitted that he was "pissed." He said it with a sense of shame for not having exercised kindness, as if he had done something wrong.

"Pissed" represented an acceptable emotion given the context, and pretending to be kind, when both the CEO and the marketing lead both knew that a gross failure had taken place, did not fit.

Many cultures show up this way—the core values simply will not assist the commercial objective of the company. Additionally, they will not help in a time of crisis and might actually hurt when needed most.

Amazingly, ineffective core values still often win the beauty contest for idiots every day.

LANGUAGE MATTERS!

My only real job working for someone else came when I was 16. It lasted three days.

A full-service gas station hired me to pump gas, and it took only ten minutes to realize my real value to the station owner was as a con man rather than a service provider. When you pulled your sofa on wheels into this station for a fill-up, I was instructed to immediately ask how much gas you wanted, and then I was required (or I would be fired) to say, "Pop the hood and I'll check your oil."

BINGO! The con was in full swing!

Notice I was not to offer, inquire, or invite, but instead to *direct* customers, many of them women, to pop the hood. This gender demographic was a key, as the service station resided in the suburbs of Detroit, where a very high percentage of men worked in the auto industry. They checked and managed their own oil levels and filters.

I was taught to go after the women only, as they rarely would have anything to do with servicing the engine, oil levels, or horsepower. They were perfect prey for a huckster.

Before giving it a thought, almost every targeted driver popped the hood, and I got to work. My boss trained me to pull the oil dipstick and purposely wipe the oil level below the fill line, all out of sight of the customer. I would then advise customers that they were "low" on oil, showing them the manipulated dipstick. Unsure, most would buy an overpriced, completely unnecessary quart of oil. Then I would get to work exposing the "dirty" filters, which get a dusty look after only a few hundred miles, long before they need to be changed. Service stations sell only overpriced, high-margin filters, and far too often, I was replacing them unnecessarily. "Your car will always run better with clean filters" was the (technically true) line I was taught.

By the end of the customer visit, voila! I had sold a tank of gas (very low profit margin), a quart of oil (80% profit margin), and an air filter (also a high profit margin). I was required to provide all of this "service," or I would lose my job!

I was fired after protesting a second time.

The lesson learned: people respond really well to a *command* rather than a request for permission.

I have never forgotten that.

CHAPTER 7

IMPROVING SCALE BY SPEAKING YOUR VALUES

"Stop. Don't. Come back."

—WILLY WONKA

THE LINGUISTIC FORMAT OF YOUR CORE VALUES MAKES A gigantic difference in your ability to capture focus and attention. Done well, core value directives allow individuals and teams to take initiative much more autonomously, as every member of the team is clear on only one rule!

THE CASE FOR ONE OVER MANY

One of the most surprising concepts reinforced by multiple scaling companies centers upon the simple idea of having only one core value directive. Yes, one, only one, for the entire company!

Wouldn't that leave out other great cultural behaviors? For a while, my coaching partners and I thought so, until we experimented with multiple companies, over many years. Here's where the idea started.

As outside coaches and advisors, we were hesitant to invest lots of money in team diagnostics completed in advance. The diagnostics never seemed to match the team that we eventually met in person.

We experimented with upgrades. We began to play games with the teams, right off the bat, offering small prizes, which triggered engagement. The first game? A pop quiz, with only one question: Name your core values in the order listed on your website.

The person who most often got the core values incorrect? The CEO.

If the CEO, who is the holder of the culture, gets the values incorrectly, what are the chances that anyone else in the organization pays any attention to them? Furthermore, with multiple values—some in direct conflict with another—how and when are team members supposed to decide which value takes precedence in any given situation, especially a crisis?

We realized that slimming down the multiple values to just one—spoken as a directive or command—clarified and simplified focus and decision-making criteria for everyone. The cultural reset started to shift behavior of team members, as everyone became much clearer as to what decisions to make, including whom to hire—based solely on following one value rather than multiple values.

Still skeptical that this actually works? Try the core value pop quiz with your team or organization. See how few of your core values people actually remember as they win this simple beauty contest for idiots.

FOUR REAL-LIFE EXAMPLES!

Meet Joanna 'Jo' Riley, the co-founder and CEO of Censia, an API-first talent intelligence company that powers modern HR technology with best-in-class talent data and ethically built HR algorithms.

Censia is Jo's fourth company, and she and the Censia team follow one core directive: "Own the outcome!" Jo has never been interested in babysitting or micromanaging her team members. Instead, she gives them the space and resources to thrive. She knows that each team member is talented and excited by the opportunity to transform one of the biggest, most important industries. That's why the entire team embraces the challenges presented every day.

"When team members 'own the outcome,' no one ever waits around to be told what to do. They take the initiative. They know the expectations, and if not, they find out," says Jo. "And then, they get to work. Rather than asking them about deadlines, we encourage team leads to ask if everyone is delivering their best work."

That question, she explains, is not meant to be an indictment but rather a quality control check. "We want everyone to be in the mindset of constant improvement. No one gets offended when we come up with a better way to do something. It simply means that we're strong enough to level up again. This is how we do our best work for our customers and our teammates, and how the work becomes the reward: every day, we sign off knowing we've done great work, learned, and improved."

Jo explains, "For this system to work, the leadership team's main objective is to hire people smarter than themselves and empower them to focus on the work at which they excel. Talented teams do better when a manager focuses the energy, not manages it. Most people only excel in 7% of the tasks they work on every day. We try to build teams where people have complementary skills, so we are a team where everyone spends as much time in their zone of genius as possible."

To keep the team focused on the mission of owning outcomes, Jo's team holds regular "Would You Sell It to Your Mother?" meetings. These meetings exist to keep everyone humble and grounded. "I don't think there is any better way to remind ourselves to own all the outcomes than to ask ourselves that one question," says Jo.

Jo and her team at Censia are scaling rapidly, with millions of API calls every day. They've grown at this rate by always owning the outcome and thinking of new and innovative ways to deliver their talent intelligence into all HR technology via APIs, quickly outpacing the growth their competitors can achieve. Censia's core directive of "Own the outcome!" empowers people to innovate every day, and its impact is evident in the impressive results they've achieved over the past two years.

Now meet Matt Carpenter, the CEO of Dealerware, a SaaS company based in Austin, Texas, that manages courtesy and rental vehicles offered to customers by franchise dealerships. If Dealerware has only one core value directive, it would sound like this: "Start with 'yes'!"

In short rather than "push ideas uphill" to a team or the entire organization, Dealerware decided to simply adopt the rule to "start with yes" and conditionally approve all ideas.

As counterintuitive as starting with yes on every idea might appear, it simplifies and limits the amount of time in meetings, because the process quickly optimizes the ideas with the most promise and invests almost no time or energy in those with little promise. One primary person "owns" the idea, and if they do not pursue the idea to completion, then the conditional approval simply falls away.

Matt realized that in most companies, most ideas need to be pushed uphill to become reality. Consider the dynamics in place when ideas have to be sold to the rest of the team, whose predisposition is not to risk the status quo. Often, that means that only the most powerful voices in any organization have any realistic chance of getting an idea approved. Multiple meetings are needed in order to consider, debate, and then reconsider. In the end, a small percentage of the ideas ever see the light of day, despite the large investment of multiple meetings with multiple teams. The process is wasteful at best, as a similar amount of time often gets invested into the good ideas as well as the bad ones.

Multiply the length of each of those meetings by the number of team members who attend, and the organizational cost to push an idea uphill becomes staggering. Most ideas then die a slow and inefficient death. As Matt suggested, "The hidden cost of all of those meetings spent on ideas that we never acted on wore out everyone, and filled calendars with meetings that held little return on involvement. People started to work longer hours, with more meetings, attended by more and more teams. It just got out of hand."

Now at Dealerware, an idea—any idea—is suggested and "owned" by one person, and it simply gets acknowledged by the rest of the team. Not praised. Not judged. Simply acknowledged, and this whole first step takes less than a minute. It might sound like this:

Phil: *I propose that we work a four-day workweek, complete our work, and close on Fridays.*

No posturing is involved; he just states the idea clearly and starts from the standpoint that "we've already conditionally agreed to this."

Now comes the ingenious part, one minute into the process. The participants in the meeting break into three- or four-person groups, for only three minutes, and their job is to "talk him out of this."

This is where the evolutionary brain protects against the idea holder's blind spots or oversights. Again, the group provides no judgments or debate about the idea or the idea holder, just a listing of possible drawbacks or unintended consequences, *ideally framed as questions* rather than as complaints. Every concern is presented in respectful, bullet-point format, without explanation. The process is quick and iterative. It might sound like this:

Team #1: *We're concerned that customer issues still occur on Fridays. Is there a remedy for that? We are concerned that it might mean the four workdays have to be elongated, and that might create backlash. Have you considered these possibilities?*

No one has to address these concerns! As the owner of the idea, Phil simply takes notes, as he is functionally responsible for furthering the idea or letting it go.

Next up, another team with additional feedback, with no duplication from the first team.

Team #2: *Could some people take days off other than Friday? If so, who covers their responsibilities on the days they are gone? Do salaries stay the same? Does the expectation and responsibility for getting your work done shift in any way? Does the idea create a dynamic where certain people still have to work on the "off" day, as their roles never take a day off?*

Again, no commentary is given, only feedback ideally in the form of questions.

Team 3: *Who decides who might take which days off, if not Fridays? Do those have to be set, or can people work one week where they take Friday off, and then start the next week with Monday off, such that they create four-day weekends? What if everyone wants the same day off?*

You get the idea. All of this occurs in a matter of minutes, and the holder of the idea simply acknowledges the feedback, thanks the teams, and usually withdraws the idea at this point in order to incorporate the feedback into a clearer proposal...if he or she chooses. In many cases the idea holder abandons the idea, and after less than ten minutes, the Dealerware team invests no more energy in it. Only the idea holder has any further investment in moving forward.

Notice that no lengthy meetings are needed. The shift in energy of the team improves. Pushing ideas uphill is no longer necessary. In the end, no idea is ever a bad idea. Most ideas get abandoned quickly, but some might just get a rework, which the team revisits anew. There is no promoting or selling ideas. Anyone can (and does) float ideas about any aspect of the organization.

For a company that runs at the pace of software development, imagine how this single directive might unleash the following:

- It could clarify actions and decision-making criteria.

- It would value ideas as a form of cultural currency.

- It would protect the company in times of a great challenge or threat. Defense first.

- It would foster an idea meritocracy rather than the loudest voice in the room.

- It would cultivate the individual wisdom of every player in the team, regardless of title.

- It could increase successful commercial outcomes. Namely, it plays offense.

- It should unite teams.

You could add your own ideas on how such a simple directive creates systems that assist in achieving a commercial outcome.

Do other cultural values exist for Matt and his team? Of course, and they follow as natural corollaries to this one core directive, because no team member anywhere loves endless hours in meetings.

Remember, the whole purpose of having only one core value directive is to build and nurture a culture that accomplishes the *commercial* objective of your company. Vetting ideas from the position of "yes, accepted" optimizes the process of decision-making, eliminates and significantly reduces the hours spent in meetings, and limits discussions on topics not yet sold. It represents a counterintuitive approach that positively affects the energy of the teams, rewards ingenuity, and creates a natural idea meritocracy.

All of this nurtured by an effective *single* core directive!

Now meet Doug Thede, the CEO of Lytho, a company that helps brand creative teams and optimize their creative operations.

Doug deployed the "one core directive" idea, when he took over as CEO in April of 2020. When hired, Doug knew the organization needed a cultural reset—a boost, if you will. The culture he inherited seemed much too passive. He heard this a lot when assessing team members: "_____ is a really good person." In Doug's listening, that translated to: "She's not very effective at her role, but we should keep her because she's a decent human being and she has worked here for a while."

That "really good person" characterization repeated itself time and time again and felt like a road to slow growth. The possibility for scaling was simply missing in such a culture. His proposed replacement: "Let people run!"

That's it.

Consider your own experience if you now worked for Doug. If you had worked in the organization for a while, might you start to run? Might you at least check your pace? If you were already running, would you run faster? Who would enjoy the pace now, since walking (or crawling, perhaps) was just too slow? Who might opt out and move on? The directive has both effects on people.

As Doug put it, "We started hiring people who wanted to run rather than walk. We started asking teams for more ambition, more speed, more impact. Some loved the shift. Others struggled, which seemed like the perfect confirmation that we were on the right track. After all, if we could walk and achieve our highest results, then we would not need to let people run."

How about prospective new hires? Would the hiring process emphasize and attract those who wanted to run and repel those who did not? Ideally, it would do both, and to everyone's satisfaction.

Now multiply the effects on teams. As Doug stated, "Does your individual contribution allow everyone around you to run, or are you the proverbial roadblock or pothole slowing things down? Managers and leaders started considering their ability to speed up the pace as one criteria for their effectiveness."

Single core directives affect every aspect of a company, most notably, hiring and onboarding new talent. You avoid bad fits based upon how you are expected to act every day rather than on ideals written on the breakroom bulletin board.

Those uncomfortable running naturally began to migrate to more suitable companies. Not many were fired. (To be fair, two leadership positions were changed in Doug's first year—not a lot.) More often, people either chose to stay and run faster or to leave on their own.

That clear separation left fewer in the middle, in "no man's land," as Doug described it. "There was a choice to make—run as a choice, or move to a more suitable organization. No threats to anyone, but an invitation to play at a different pace and with a different attitude. It took a while to shift the organization, and the results started showing up."

For any decision or project, the sole criteria to consider is, does this create the platform to run, walk, or drag our feet? For our team? For our customers? For our overall future prospects?

"Running meant that we moved with freedom, we moved with responsibility, and we moved with the proper urgency. Here, running is not only speed but an attitude and a philosophy. We want our teammates and our customers to operate at their highest and best use. Letting people run will do that. People who want to take responsibility and solve problems don't want to be micromanaged; it stifles them. Letting them run provides them more opportunities to grow and succeed—while making them happier and contributing more value."

Play defense first. Engage the same directive to play offense.

The results started to show up quickly. Doug acquired another company in his first year, buying a specific technology that his firm did not hold. Doug continues to deploy this directive with newly acquired team members, as well as original hires, with drastically improved results!

Finally, meet Steven Moy, CEO of Barbarian, a branding agency associated with transforming the messages and images of companies and movements. Barbarian is a regional firm rather than a boutique agency or a gigantic player. Steven has his entire team committed to one simple core directive: "Create the future faster!"

If we use the principles already suggested, let's put this sole directive to the test.

Barbarian competes against much larger agencies with significantly larger employee head counts and budgets. Barbarian realized if it were to win against these larger competitors, it would most likely win primarily based upon speed....or lose because of lack of speed. Specifically, does Barbarian respond to its customers more quickly? Does it engage more quickly? Does it book contracts before the larger, slower agencies ever get moving? Does it create a gigantic win before the other agencies fully engage in the race?

Speed can kill. From a defensive point of view, lack of speed, it turns out, was the real killer.

Steven and his team are insanely talented. The team has little room for inexperienced players. They compete in a market that adheres a bit to the old saying, "No one ever got fired by hiring IBM." In the branding world, that translates to, "Hire the better-known entity." Barbarian is often the unconventional choice for an agency because it is much lesser known, but customers continue to thrive by hiring Barbarian.

When Barbarian moves quickly, creating the future faster for its clients, its creativity gets showcased, engaged, and enhanced before the bigger competitors have time to move through their processes. Since Steven has only experienced talent on his roster, the team who competes against the larger firm is usually "pound for pound" more talented, as Barbarian has no B and C players. It simply cannot afford to keep such players. Talented employees come to Barbarian because they want to play a big game, without the politics of a larger firm. They want to beat the Goliaths in the industry. They want to outplay, outhustle, and outcreate the larger competition.

At Barbarian, those same players get to play in a fast-paced, big-stakes game. If you are on the team, you will absolutely play! You will learn way more quickly. You will progress in your career more quickly. Steven put it this way: "People who want to play at Barbarian want to play right away, not sit for a year or two as a junior player. We give them meaningful work to do, as we believe in learning by doing, not by watching. If you want to learn, then your contributions will not only be welcomed, but required! You'll see the direct impact of your contribution and take pride in the difference you made on any client project. The larger agencies provide a safer playing field, so people who believe in themselves come to work with us. We want them only if they want to play. That process suits everyone well!"

Let's check the strategy of Barbarian's directive, namely, play defense first.

Creating the future faster protects Barbarian against much larger competitors, by responding more quickly, bidding more quickly, creating more quickly, and, ultimately, delivering more quickly. This hustle delivers on its capability and follows the company's directive, such that it excels and scales. In short, playing defense first (that is, getting the contract more quickly and more responsively) and exercising creativity are both designed to win!

Imagine now that you are a talented player in the branding field, considering a position at Barbarian. At the first interview, would the idea of "creating the future faster" singularly color your conversation with the Barbarian team? Would it scare you or attract you? Might it be exactly what you have been looking for? Would it repel you?

Effective and clear core directives achieve this by their structure and simplicity! It would be difficult to move too quickly at Barbarian, if you are taking care of the clientele and your teammates.

Do your values lead directly to scaling? If you're looking to speed up growth, consider replacing your current values with only one customized core directive that will ensure commercial success.

KEY LEARNING POINTS

1. Most team members cannot pass a simple test to state the company's agreed-upon cultural values.

2. Most companies hold way too many core values. When a crisis hits and decisive action is needed most, team members do not know which values to deploy.

3. Directives (or commands) tell people what to do and can be designed to assist in accomplishing your commercial vision.

4. Holding (far) fewer core directives simplifies and clarifies activities for everyone in the organization.

5. Creating a sole core directive forces your team to "get it right" as holding only one presents a much more challenging task than holding many.

As I said before, scaling tends to eat culture for breakfast, lunch, dinner, and late-night snacks. One core directive is just one tool to accomplish scale. Now let's play with more structural and cultural tools to help in your scaling.

SCALING PRACTICE #3: SETTING ONE CORE DIRECTIVE

If you want to improve the impact of your highest value, and set yourself up to scale much more easily, follow these five steps to create one core directive:

Step #1: Speak all values in the directive form. Essentially, begin the articulation of the directive with an *action* verb. (Note: If the directive needs further explanation, it's not clear.)

Step #2: Connect the proposed core value (spoken as a directive) only to your highest *commercial* outcome or mission. Generally, that means that your core value (for example, the word "honesty") would never appear in the directive.

Step #3: Start with a version of your directive that assists the most when your company has its worst possible day. Once you have it stated powerfully to play defensively, then check to see whether that same directive assists you to grow rapidly as well. If not, consider a different value or different language.

Step #4: Keep your directive short. The fewer words, the better.

Step #5: Try out your proposed core value in different ways. Interview some candidates using it. Use it to perform an employee review or solve a customer issue. You'll know if it's right when solving problems becomes easier.

Step #6: Deploy only *one* directive! This adds power, as you will have to "get it right." Customize the directive specifically to achieve your commercial objective. Multiple core directives dilute focus and compete for your team members' attention, usually when the team needs clarity and focus most.

Did you notice what all six steps have in common? Yup. They are all directives.

PART 3

MORE TOOLS TO HELP YOU SCALE

CHAPTER 8

DOES TALENT OR CULTURE FIT SCALE BETTER? (HINT: IT'S NOT EVEN CLOSE...)

"Doing easily what others find difficult is talent; doing what is impossible with talent is genius."

—HENRI FRÉDÉRIC AMIEL

THE MOST DIVISIVE QUESTION ASKED OF EVERY CEO INTER-viewed for this book was, "If you had to hire 100% for talent or 100% for culture, which would you do in order to scale?"

The question brought forth three very distinct answers:

1. "Always hire for culture fit first!"

2. "Always hire for talent first!"

3. That faraway look that indicated the CEO had never really thought about it before.

Three out of four respondents fell into the last category, which seems telling. Regardless of your own response, every company effectively hires for both. That's pretty easy to prove, as your talent-first approach most likely would hold at least some minimal safeguards against hiring people who proudly reveal in the first interview that they, say, own 53 cats or collect large-caliber, automatic rifles and large hunting knives.

Only one answer holds a significantly better chance to scale, so if two of three possible answers clearly lose out, is it talent or culture fit that wins?

THE REAL ISSUE: NATURE VERSUS NURTURE

When pressing 275 CEOs with the same question, only one in four answered quickly and definitively, which is to say that the other 75% really had not considered exactly what hiring strategy they deploy in order to scale.

Could this rate of indecisiveness mirror the failure rate of companies? Does it make a difference in the rate of scaling if you focus solely on talent and then build a culture around it? Or if you do the reverse, build a great culture first and then attract the necessary talent to that culture?

As with many questions, the "talent or culture" query posed might not be so helpful. If you are looking for an edge in scaling, try this question instead: "Is it simpler to teach bad-ass talent or to teach highly desired behaviors you want in your company?" Alternatively, you could ask, "Is great talent more innate than desired behaviors, or is the reverse true?"

If you observe young children, you might notice that some kids are just more proficient at playing the piano or ice skating, even with comparable lessons and practice. Does that signal that talent comes more from nature than nurture? Are those same kids all demonstrating primarily the values their classroom teacher espouses, or do they more closely follow the values espoused in their homes?

In the end, which is easier to learn, values or talent?

To answer the tougher questions, you have to look at some underlying premises that the culture-first camp holds:

1. If we hire first for talent, our culture will suffer.

Is this really true? Is your culture so delicate that highly talented people will show up as behavioral misfits or outright assholes? How often do talented people deteriorate or wreck cultures, simply by holding or demonstrating outstanding talent?

It's easy enough to answer that question for yourself. Is the most talented person in your organization also the largest cultural problem in your organization? How about the second most talented person? Unless the five most talented people on your team are also the five worst culture fits (or outright assholes), this argument falls apart very quickly. Oddly, many CEOs hold the belief as truth.

This idea that supreme talent will hurt culture feels much like the unexamined case for gender or racial bias that has been used far too long.

> **Two-Day-Old Sushi:** Believing that hiring for talent first means you will have a company full of assholes, as if all talented people are assholes. Talented people are...well, people. Like any group of people, a very small percentage might be classified as assholes, and you most likely will weed them out.

2. Our culture is unique.

Really? If that were the case, then a search for companies with your exact same core values would result in discovering that all of them are "world-class," or have award-winning cultures. Do they? And do their awards amount to scaling victories that stakeholders, team members, and customers will celebrate?

Most companies draw their operating core values from essentially the same play list, often copying companies who have gone public or have drawn media attention for their great culture. Do the same values ensure your own winning edge? Will you win a culture award too?

3. Our award-winning culture will win over a dumpster fire of a culture every time.

Is that really true? After all, some culturally bankrupt companies (WeWork, Uber, Oracle) have created very successful companies, despite very poorly rated work environments.

In our research, cultures found anywhere on the spectrum—from an outright dumpster fire to best in class—scaled. The award-winning cultures held statistically no advantage in the ability to scale, and by a small margin, actually scaled at a worse rate than did companies that did not win a darn thing for their culture. The award-winning culture companies did retain team members longer than those who did not focus on culture, by approximately 21%.

Perhaps, it is more enjoyable to work at those culturally healthier companies. But if given the choice to scale, but only in a company with a culture that is not "award winning," would you place your bet on a company with a higher level of talent as the primary focus instead? In the end, that's the bet you place every day—that either talent or culture gives you the better chance to win your commercial objectives. It's a gigantic bet, and one worth winning.

4. Our funding source will reward us for winning commercially or culturally.

Are you sure about that? Funders are rarely attracted to organizations that do not focus on attracting top-tier talent. A strong focus on hiring and developing talent creates a culture of its own, where talent is honored, deployed, and compensated. You'll work side-by-side with people more talented than you are, and you'll strengthen and refine your craft. You will be challenged and rewarded every single day. If that prospect excites you, there are companies that you will absolutely love— because they engage your top talent and expect you to play at a high level every single day.

Could the same be said if 'culture add' was substituted for talent in the statements above?

YMCA VERSUS RANDOM TALENT

The "employee experience" approach so prevalent in today's business climate is a bit like thinking your YMCA Tuesday night co-ed volleyball team would win against any three random members of the US Olympic team because your team has played together for years and has great "chemistry and culture."

You'll lose. Badly. Every time, even with your full squad of six against their three.

Talent works like that, even if the three random US Olympians have never played together before. They might not agree on a team cheer or their uniform colors (how about red, white, and blue?), but their superior talent will act like a giant can of whoop-ass against you and your super cohesive "great culture" team who gets along really well...at least until you're losing badly.

Now let's meet Art Pravato, the CEO of T-Metrics, a leader in providing highly-secure, next-generation contact center software to mission critical users in government, military, healthcare, education, finance, and other countless organizations around the world.

When Art took over as CEO in 2020, the team was doing "well enough," but not well enough to scale. Art started to assess the current talent, recruit, and enhance the talent of existing employees in their individual roles.

Here's what Art outlined very quickly as some of the reasons he and his company hire for the "top 1% talent" instead of worrying too much about their culture.

In Art's words: "We recognize that culture appears primarily as an *outcome*, not a catalyst. T-Metrics needs specialists, engineers, and extremely talented people to achieve the rate of growth we strive for. If the people we hire are "top 1%," they do not alter the culture much, except to spur team members to even higher levels of performance. Talent drives talent. Talent attracts more (and better) talent. Talent provides a focal point to rally around. If you are hired to play on that top team, you love it and play all out. If you're not a great talent fit, you will tend to move on.

"New people—talented or not—alter our culture in one specific way, often because they challenge everyone to do even better quality work. Onboarding a great talent into an atmosphere of already existing talent makes a difference, by making everyone better...or at least not slowing anyone down."

Organizations that mistake culture as a primary catalyst to scale, rather than as an outcome, miss out on talent that might not look like the model cultural fit. Art and his team realize that in its simplest form, culture represents what you reward and punish. Art and his team reward talent.

Art also noticed more clearly than ever in the pandemic that attempting to "vet people for our culture" is futile, since interview candidates are almost always on their best behavior, with scripted answers to most interview questions. It's a bit like a polite first date. No controversial opinions are aired, and only the most positive answers and even scripted stories are heard. Because the candidates have never worked at T-Metrics, their interviews represent the best-behaved versions of themselves you might ever meet, as opposed to the person who shows up on day one. Art and his team can handle behavioral quirks much more easily than talent issues.

An improved standard for judging a new hire might sound like this: "What happens to our intended culture (since culture is an outcome) when a new hire has worked here for three months? Are we a better organization for the hire, or worse? Are we more capable? Are we more likely to succeed at our commercial outcome? Are we engaging our team members more as a result of this new team member?"

Only then will you know more concretely if the new hire is a poor, decent, or terrific fit. If your basic cultural rule is to hire for top 1% talent, then the impact on the organization centers solely upon how well new hires measure up to the tasks at hand. How do they impact results or speed? What new possibilities have appeared because of their top talent? Does the expression of their individual talents allow for others to express their own talents more fully?

In short, it's just way more effective to hire primarily for talent, and then (very occasionally) fire team members for attitude or extremely poor behavior. This best practice of scaling companies proved to be the most impactful *counterintuitive* practice, namely *hire solely for top talent without regard for your culture.*

Of the companies we looked at (over five thousand) who had reached a designation as "scaling," three out of four were talent-focused, and only one in four were culture-focused. Like your favorite sports team or philharmonic orchestra, the best talent generally outperforms inferior talent.

It seems illogical at best, downright arrogant at worst, to think that your team members are shaped by your company's values, to the degree that they can now grow a company better than they could have before they were taught your values.

Since knowing behavioral or psychological factors in advance is impossible, Art and his team at T-Metrics instead focus intently on hiring the best talent. Ironically, this idea equals a very strong cultural statement. Imagine that you are confident of your talent and that you are looking for a team that will require you to excel, learn, and grow in your role. You will make the people around you better, and they will engage, challenge, and improve your game every day. Does that frighten you enough to decline the opportunity, or does it compel you to want to join Art's team?

> **Beauty Contest for Idiots:** Assuming that new hires will be reshaped or influenced by your core values or culture. By a young age, most people's personalities (including values) are well developed, and your culture will not alter them. They might focus more on the values that you espouse, but they will not shift from their own values and be reshaped by yours.

With a focus on attracting and hiring the top talent, T-Metric's clear obsession has a designed effect of scaring away people who are intimidated by the prospect of excelling. Again, nothing wrong with wanting a great culture. We all do. But in the end, a culture focused almost solely on talent holds one flavor, and a culture that centers upon behavioral attributes or employee experience holds quite a different flavor.

Harsh? Perhaps. What we found from the fastest growing companies is that talent becomes a much better predictor of commercial success than does award-winning culture. Those attempting to play and win "the culture game" have this premise:

1. Build a great culture.

2. Showcase that culture to attract people we like better and get along with, ideally with great talent.

3. Those better cultural fits will then scale the company.

The theory seems reasonable and makes some sense, but if you hire first for culture, that becomes the higher focus than does commercial success. Hence, for the same reason that any three US Volleyball Olympians can crush your YMCA volleyball team, even if the Olympians have never played together before, the talent in other organizations can predictably crush your award-winning culture. That reason also explains why a dumpster fire of a culture with talent can succeed commercially, whereas a limited talent company with a great culture fails.

In the end, an award-winning culture attracts people looking for an employee experience. A talent-focused organization attracts those who want to be challenged in their skill mastery first, and that tends to attract others who also hold top talent. Substandard players need not apply—regardless of their culture add.

Culture also can attract many who believe that it is the company's job to inspire them, treat them well, and reward them handsomely...as a precondition of doing any work. Talent-driven teams, on the other hand, tend to work in a meritocracy, where if you provide great value, you get rewarded and advance. These two paradigms are not cast in concrete but exist instead on opposite ends of a spectrum. Would you rather go where your talent is engaged, challenged, and rewarded, or where you are honored for how well you fit in culturally?

Ironically, all companies are running a culture and talent game simultaneously, dictated by which option the CEO and leadership team embraces. For talent-only/talent-first companies, the culture is dictated by you and all of your super-talented peers. For culture-first companies, your ability to appeal to the hiring team, based upon believing what the company believes, dictates your ability to be hired, promoted, and honored.

Neither model is better. They are just different. Which model would you "bet the ranch" on with a $10M venture investment?

KEY LEARNING POINTS

1. Talent attracts more talent. Culture attracts more culture. Choose to become a talent-first or culture-first organization, if you would like to scale faster.

2. Talent more likely emanates from genetics (nature). Behaviors more likely emanate from environment (nurture).

3. Award-winning cultures and dumpster-fire cultures can both scale. Rarely do limited talent companies ever scale.

Overwhelmingly, talent succeeds in scaling by a three-to-one margin. That's not to say that culture cannot scale, so let's explore how to do just that.

SCALING PRACTICE #4: HIRING EXCLUSIVELY FOR TALENT

The premise is simple. Great talent will win out against a great culture, by more than a three-to-one margin. Hence, hiring exclusively for top talent becomes a much safer scaling bet. Your stakeholders and investors will reward you only for a commercial success, so increasing your odds of success could rest on this notion.

Step #1: Create a hiring process that focuses on talent exclusively. The net effect will be to attract those looking to excel and grow their talent and to repel those looking for primarily an employee-experience company.

Step #2: Redesign your hiring questions and process to focus on high achievement, lifetime learning, mastery, and achieving challenging goals.

Step #3: Invite candidates to invest a day with a team they might work on. This will attract or repel them from joining your organization.

Step #4: Enact a thirty-day rule. If any new hire appears to be a cultural disaster in their treatment of other team members, fire them immediately. Make this rule clear before you hire. Then notice how few people you fire for inappropriate behavior.

CHAPTER 9

CULTURE FIT SCALING

"With the right people, culture, and values, you can create great things."

—TRICIA GRIFFITH

As I took on the idea of figuring out what makes a company scale faster, it became very apparent that talent and culture fit were the leading options.

I wish I had one sold book for every CEO I interviewed who vehemently insisted that his or her company's "amazing culture" stood as the foundation for the company's pace of scaling. The majority of the 275+ CEOs I interviewed claimed that culture scales much better than does talent. I already had lots of data that proved otherwise, but that doesn't mean that no companies can scale using a culture-first approach. Though the odds do not favor this approach, many are pursuing it, so I looked into it.

Ironically, my research showed almost identical results as the results from my research on the talent-first approach...but in reverse. Most CEOs (73%) believed that a culture-first approach offers the best chance to scale. However, for those companies that actually have achieved scale, 76% of the CEOs attributed their success to their top talent rather than to their culture, even when offered both choices side by side.

YOUR COMPANY'S CULTURE

Ask CEOs to describe their company culture, and this often occurs:

- They espouse company culture as the main reason for their success.

- When asked, they can list their highest core values or their operating principles only with some help, since they do not remember all of them.

- They list essentially the same values as other companies in their industry, some of which are succeeding and some of which are failing miserably.

It seems clear that given the core values often were not even fully known by the CEO, that the reason people are drawn to the culture-first approach is perhaps because it simply feels better or maybe works better for recruiting, not because it is a proven method for success. Still, companies absolutely can scale with a culture-first or talent-first approach. The odds favor betting on talent, but for those who like the culture-first approach, let's discuss it.

THE HIDDEN TRUTHS ABOUT ANY CULTURE

Ask people to describe the actualities of their own family culture, and the stories range from hilarious to downright scary. Dad's seething resentment colors everything else that occurs in the family. The youngest sibling has been given a free pass to coast, while the rest of us had to make our own way. Mom's always the peacemaker.

Your own family culture takes its own form, often with little resemblance between the declared ideals and the actual rules. Nowhere in any family do the leaders declare that their true core values are *resentment and entitlement*, even though their repeated actions over time support those values every day. Predictable outcomes from those active behaviors follow, not always for the betterment of the household. The family learns to live with Dad's seething resentment as a constant, knowing the consequences and penalties connected to it.

Your work team works much the same. Start with the premise that your company culture equals the *outcome* of what you repeatedly do, as opposed to being *dictated by your highest intentions*. If all cultures—company or family—succeeded in their intentions, there would be far more successes in business and far fewer broken families.

Neither could be further from the truth. The overwhelming percentage of companies eventually fail, and divorce rates indicate more than half of homes are broken. If culture-first was the espoused strategy to succeed, then did the culture fail, or something else? Rarely do postmortems on failed companies include "toxic culture" as the reason for failure. Generally, more commercial reasons kill companies, like lack of funding, poor product design, poor execution, or lack of strong leadership.

THE NEW ARRIVAL OR NEW HIRE

If you have children or have friends with children, you know the *outcome produced* by the arrival of a first child. Before, you have two people with, most likely, an adult(ish) lifestyle that includes socializing with friends, working out, and eating at restaurants. Then a seven-pound major disruption arrives in the form of wrecked sleep, constant care, and the occasional delightful behavior—which makes it all worth it. In no way, shape, or form does the culture of that home ever remain the same. The home culture equals the outcome of the effects that the new arrival has on all of the family members.

Now add a second child, and perhaps a third. Throw in a puppy for good measure. Despite best cultural intentions, the culture of the family adapts and changes from accommodating the quiet and reserved first kid to also accommodating the "live-wire" second kid and the puppy that has to be walked and cared for. Life evolves to take care of the diverse inhabitants rather than the inhabitants changing to adapt their personalities to the well-designed culture of the home.

Even with very clearly stated and understood house rules, every real-life situation alters the environment and, mostly, the people remain the same. Just ask fully grown "live-wire" kids. They are most likely adult versions of themselves at two years old (read: taller). Their home culture did not alter their personalities at all! In most cases, their actions flavored and shaped the family culture much more than the reverse.

Your work team acts the same. You hire an introvert, a competitor, and a pleaser, and the collection of individuals adjusts slightly every time new personalities enter the company. When the competitive spirit in the newly hired salesperson gently evolves, the values of the company (which most likely do not include "competition" as a core value) might begin dulling that same salesperson. Most often, no one can dull the part of the salesperson who competes fiercely for every deal, in much the same way that attempting to quiet live-wires can make them more lively, not less.

Remember, we're looking here to scale. So let's create some rules for scaling via the culture-fit route:

Rule #4: Remember that your culture exists as an outcome rather than as a catalyst of behaviors.

Rarely do people alter who they are due to your stated cultural values. They arrived to your team with their own personalities and values pretty much baked in.

Let's go back to the puppy example. If you've ever considered adopting a puppy, much like onboarding a prospective employee, your visits to the pound are under very controlled circumstances. You and your kids visit the pound, where attention-starved, adorable puppies await their turns to audition. They're cute and friendly, perhaps they jump up and lick you with enthusiasm, and you bring home the perfect choice—until they turn out to be "chewers." They chew your shoes. They chew the couch. They chew the kids' backpacks. They chew everything! That detail was simply not apparent at the pound!

Problem is, by now, the kids love the dog, and you might not survive a vote on whether to keep the puppy or you as a breadwinner. The *outcome* is a modified culture of your home: you begin to alter rules, attitudes, and behaviors—simply to limit the damage to both your shoes and your sanity!

Now shift to interviewing candidates with the idea of vetting for a culture fit. Far be it from me to imply that your hires hang out in kennels, but essentially, think of hiring interviews as a virtual version of the pound. Your prospects have great recommendations. Years of experience. Great education. Professional profile pictures. Perhaps as an added bonus, they aspire to the same core values as your company holds!

Every prospective employee, just like every puppy, acts in a way that will get them hired. Your puppy did not come with a "full disclosure" indicating it would chew everything in sight. Neither does any prospective team member, so "vetting" for your culture is not only inefficient (read: wastes lots of time and money) but is also nearly impossible to get right under the choreographed circumstances of an interview. Besides, if your team could not write down their own core values in a pop quiz, how could they possibly vet a candidate effectively for those same core values?

The reality is that you'll know what puppy or employee you actually brought home after about a month.

Rule #5: Hire only for culture-adds rather than culture-fits.

First, fire the very few people who live too far outside of what you and your team tolerates in terms of attitudes and behaviors. Then hire a few new people using a culture-add approach.

Hiring for a culture-add allows differing values and opinions, but only those that would add value and perspective to your organization. For example, if a team is passive, hiring an intense new team leader who naturally embraces accountability, takes initiative, and challenges people might fall outside of your company core values, but it would turn around the struggling team. At this point in the discussions, the CEOs generally would declare that they should at least "weed out the assholes" to protect the company culture (otherwise known as the "no asshole rule").

I agree completely, if only it were possible. Here's a generally accurate tendency for assholes: rarely do they view themselves as such! And since you so proudly laid out your core values on

your website or in advanced conversations, it's not terribly difficult for asshole prospects to present themselves in the manner
that *you* have dictated—espousing, or at least accepting, your
aspirational core values.

Whether you're hiring for culture or talent, firing assholes early
on in their employment is actually much easier and cheaper
than attempting to weed them out in advance. Consider your
own team—how many people have you terminated based upon
their views? How many have you terminated because they did
not do acceptable work?

Consider this, however, before firing someone who does
not fit in: are they really detrimental to your culture, or are
they just different? Team members who are overly intense,
shy, or hesitant hold behaviors that most likely show up in
direct opposition to the majority of the team. Would their
differences show up in full color when intensity, shyness, or
hesitancy is needed most? If you hire an ultra-intense head
of sales, will that operating mode make the sales team more
effective? If so, then can your culture adapt to having "extremes" connected to specific roles?

Truth is, no one complains much about a leader who is big on
empathy, since empathy generally offends few. When a senior
leader lacks patience or tolerance for slow results, does that
more effectively spur the team on than does empathy? If so,
perhaps the leader is not an asshole, but instead stands out
as extreme in a manner that serves as a catalyst for much-
needed results.

Extreme talents or cultural attributes do not assholes make. Get rid of only those who exhibit truly unacceptable behaviors or attitudes.

Rule #6: Expect great talent to come with quirks, personalities, and extremes.

When do you fire for poor attitudes or divisive personalities? It's a great question, and when considering scaling or building for growth, the one difference between a quirky person and a terrorist is: *recruiting.*

If team members, especially new ones, hold views, opinions, attitudes, and especially talents that do not match the rest of the team, that is neither good nor bad. Focus on the *outcomes* and catalytic effects of those differences. Those team members almost always see things differently, and that might be why they got hired. If the company had hired yet another person who thinks and acts in the same way as the rest of the team, it would have been hiring for a culture-fit, but what the team needed to improve was a culture-add.

Once employees start *recruiting* others to their negative point of view, however, then they cross over into possible terrorist classification. Here are common examples:

- Two weeks into his new employment, an employee whispers to a coworker in an all-hands meeting, "Do you think this CEO really knows what the hell he is doing?"

- In a team lunch, an employee tells a dirty or off-color joke to the group surrounding her. This is a more subtle form of recruiting in which a person attempts to develop a tribe of people who laugh at the same things (usually inappropriate or divisive humor).

- An employee berates the high school intern for getting his coffee drink wrong. Essentially, he is recruiting people to his idea that he has the right to treat poorly people who hold a lower position in the organization.

These types of activities reveal a person's actual views. When people behave in this way, they are most likely looking for confirmation that their actions fit in the organization. Their behavior is an early indication that they will most likely treat coworkers, vendors, and customers poorly.

When anyone on the team moves from quirky or extreme into recruiting mode, consider terminating them, immediately— not because they are different, but because they exhibit attitudes and behaviors that are out of bounds and would wreck any culture if copied by many.

Rule #7: Embrace the values people hold and marry their values with your company's values. Almost always, they will fit pretty well.

UNLUCKY SEVENS

When you've filled out customer service surveys with a numerical scale, have you ever noticed that the majority of your responses fall on the far ends of the spectrum? People tend to rate service as either really horrible (1 on the scale) or really great (a perfect 10).

Consider the breakdown of a 1-10 rating spectrum. Anything under 5 is a clear message that the service provider needs improvement. A rating of 6-9 is positive, but not necessarily perfect. A 6, for example, implies that there are still further improvements that would make your experience better. As the customer, you might have clear suggestions, even if you choose not to share them with the vendor. Perhaps the vendor simply did not hit the mark as well as you would have liked.

What about 7s? They represent an odd spot—"pretty good," if expressed in words. Not exemplary. Not stellar. Rating a 7 is a bit conflict-averse—you don't want to fight about the service falling short (it's just too much work), but the service provider is not worthy of referrals.

TALENT AND CULTURE 7S

Whether you are scaling for culture or scaling for talent, consider the impact of a "pretty good" culture fit, or a "pretty talented" team member. It's no man's land. A 7 team member mutes or slows down the bad-ass talent (9s and 10s) because a

7 can keep up sometimes, but not always. A 7 in talent could not lead a team of talents who are 9s and 10s—at least not in any kind of meritocracy—because everyone on the team knows that the 7 does not have a reputation for excellence.

Again, this scenario emphasizes the importance of making a strategic decision well in advance of hiring. Make a structural decision (organizational structure) prior to building out teams. Then decide what your teams need and hire solely for talent or solely for culture-fit. Hiring for both equals hiring for neither.

SEVEN AND SEVENS

Now consider the "both" people. They are fairly talented, at about a 7 level, and they fit the culture pretty well, again at the 7 level, meaning they are not quite full-fledged ambassadors for the culture. They are leading or collaborating with some people who possess much more talent (probably prominent players, due to their impact) and some people who love, embrace, and represent the company culture very well. How can this "7 & 7" inspire greater results from team members who are much more talented, or worse yet, better culture-adds?

In the end, super-talented team members (9s and 10s) are actually *twice as talented* as 7s, which can cause trouble in teams when 7 leaders cannot keep up with their 9 and 10 team members. The same goes for extreme culture-adds. When the most ardent supporters of the culture outpace the team leader, problems simply arise.

In the end, the 7 & 7 leader ends up "pretty good" overall but not good enough in either aspect. This absolutely frustrates both the talent and culture-fit 9s and 10s because it negates their expertise and their ability to fit into the culture. The bigger damage usually occurs on the talent side, as those very talented people want to play at a much higher level than the team leader is capable of. If they feel like they have to drag the leader along, then they either silo or, worse yet, just leave. Or they play at the pace of the leader and get bored. None of these options is optimal, especially for teams that are scaling.

This scenario is a wet blanket; it acts as a tax, of sorts, levied on the team and the entire organization! If the 7 & 7 leader stays in power, the best employees in both culture and talent tend to change teams (if allowable) or take their talents elsewhere. Rarely does "pretty good" scale or grow organizations.

Pick culture first and hire great culture-adds, or pick talent first and hire only the most talented people in the market. Either way, be sure to hire the 9s and 10s—because "lucky 7s" are anything but.

KEY LEARNING POINTS

1. Culture shows up in the form of outcomes. Design your culture backward, starting with the outcomes you would like to create.

2. Culture-adds will grow your company much better than culture-fits. Hire only culture-adds.

3. Whether hiring for talent first or culture first, always fire quickly for attitudes that do not grow your team.

4. 9s and 10s in talent and 9s and 10s in culture fit are actually twice as capable as 7s.

5. Team leaders who are less of a culture fit and have less talent than their much more talented team players tend to stifle innovation and results.

6. Pick a platform (talent or culture) and hire for extremes. Middle ground is no man's land.

By now, you should have decided to build for talent or for culture. Next up, are there core values that successfully scale better than others? We found them, and chances are, you might want to borrow some. Let's do that together in the next chapter.

CHAPTER 10

DO YOUR VALUES SCALE BETTER THAN MINE?

"Values hold the team together, provide stability for the team to grow upon, measure the team's performance, give direction and guidance and attract like-minded people."

—JOHN MAXWELL

IF YOU'RE LIKE MOST PARENTS, YOU ARE PROUD OF YOUR KIDS. Me too.

Honestly now, are your kids *really* the smartest in math? Is their musical or athletic talent world-class? How about their first baby pictures, posted online. Cutest baby ever? Or is your bias clouded by your pride of parenthood?

Parents tend to be biased. Perhaps we all share that trait.

CEOs speak a bit in the same way about their culture and their foundational core values. Look online at the published core values for any five companies, and you'll see a lot of the same themes.

Might your core values equate to the entrepreneurial equivalent of an ugly baby? More importantly, if your company baby is ugly, will anyone have the courage to tell you? After all, an ugly baby is an ugly baby, regardless of whether anyone actually has the courage (or nerve) to tell you.

WHERE MEDIOCRITY BEGINS: EXPECTED VALUES

Of all the companies I researched, I found that only a small percentage were scaling (meaning, remember, that year after year their growth rates have been 50% faster than the rest of their industries). I started to notice a trend: the values of the higher-growth companies came from a very different bucket than most of the companies who experienced average or below-average growth.

That realization got our research team to wondering, "Do certain core values scale more effectively than do others?" Or in the parlance of grade school, "Can my core values beat up your core values?" Rather than starting a rock fight or schoolyard tussle, we started to identify the common values that most (failing) companies held. We call most of these "expected values." In short, you and your company get no real credit for holding them, nor does your culture improve. And then we proposed putting the values head-to-head in a more valuable fight...a fight for an increase in rate of growth. See if you recognize any of these common values that provide the foundation of your team's culture:

- Family—Proof? Pick three family members you would permanently ban from your company.

- Creativity—Required in every company.

- Unity—Often shows up as "consensus." (Lemmings unite too.)

- Integrity—Try NOT having integrity and succeeding at anything.

- Hard work—As if you and your team have cornered the market on this trait.

- Loyalty—We pay you, for goodness' sake.

- Honesty—The least effective core value created. Just check the weight on your license.

- Open(ness)—How do we measure what level is appropriate?

- Fairness—Would you remain with a company that treats you unfairly?

These values sound great, but lack any power or effectiveness. They may be very well-suited for your golden retriever, but they won't help you succeed in your business or even your family. Problem is, they really do *sound* valuable, so companies fall in love with these in much the same way as they fall in love with golden retriever puppies.

When looking to weed out ineffective values, ask yourself these three simple questions:

1. Without holding this value, could I hold a job?

2. Without holding this value, could I enter into personal or professional partnerships?

3. Without holding this value, could I have any friends?

BEAUTY CONTEST FOR GOLDEN RETRIEVERS

In 2007, I foolishly invested in a company with these simple values: open, honest, and fair. Ask yourself the three questions above, and you probably will come to the same conclusion I eventually did: no wonder we all got conned!

Start with *honesty*. Without it, there's no real way to hold a job, have any friends, or make any partnerships.

Now *fair*. If I were consistently *un*fair, I'd have trouble holding a job, making friends, or entering into partnerships. It would be much easier to get into arguments, lawsuits, and entanglements.

Finally, *open(ness)*. If I were closed-minded, I'd also find it extremely difficult to hold a job, have any friends, or enter partnerships.

You and I are expected to be open, honest, and fair. In the end, when companies extoll the virtue of values meant for golden retrievers, they have essentially built the foundation of their companies on wet dog hair.

If the following list seems mean-spirited, remember, we're only looking to find differentiators that help scale. We offer some "upgraded" core values that will drive much more effective behavior.

AND THE WINNERS ARE....

One year at the Oscars, a winner playfully thanked the other nominees for losing, without whom the winner could not have won. The crowd laughed, and finally, one decent speech came out of an otherwise boring evening.

Winners do need losers, now, don't they? Well, we propose only the most effective values that might help you scale more effectively.

Transparency—Perhaps no core value scales better. Why? Because without transparency, companies default to what they call honesty, radical candor, or brutal honesty.

Transparency shows up like this: *Tell the entire truth, up front, regardless of the consequences.*

Try this for yourself. How many major issues in your company would have been cleared up much faster, cheaper, and with less disruption if all players simply exercised transparency? It starts with the CEO, who most likely will make as many bad calls or decisions as anyone in the company. Do you fire the CEO for every mistake, or disclose mistakes fully, regroup, and move forward?

The power of this value stems from the fact that human beings are custom-built to handle all kinds of serious challenges. We thrive on it. The key to unlocking the full power of any team is being up front about the situation quickly and completely, as that jumpstarts the process toward solving the challenge. No blame. Someone takes full responsibility, and the team then takes over to begin correcting.

Just ask Carolyn Parent, CEO of Conveyer, a New York City-area-based company that transforms static, inflexible product instructions into dynamic mobile experiences that build trust, enhance customer service, and create new revenue opportunities for manufacturers. Conveyer is not her first rodeo; Carolyn successfully built and sold LiveSafe, and transparency was a key reason for the big success.

In her own words: "People are hard-wired to know everything, without editing. We get information in real time, so why would we thrive with less than full transparency from the team we live and work with for years? Teammates all need to feel the great parts of the roller-coaster ride of growing a business and get the anxiety too. In order to accomplish that, they need all the data points available, not just some. Information on capital, customers, pipeline, product development status—all these data points are part of the big picture of growing a company. Not everyone can take all detailed parts of the ups and downs every day, but teammates need to feel informed and be part of the ride."

At LiveSafe, Carolyn found that transparency acted as the catalyst for outcomes that facilitated much faster growth and much better employee retention. Her hierarchy was: transparency supports authenticity, which in turn builds trust and safety. "That formula scales much better than does keeping people fully or partially in the dark. Doing so signals that you do not trust them with data."

So, what did Carolyn share and with whom? As she said, "Almost anything! With my Board, they were never surprised, as they knew information in real time—good or bad. If thrown a curve ball, we could react and agree on a course of action, as we needed no time to get up to speed. That worked really well, even if at times, the news reported was not always positive. I just don't believe in steering or managing my Board. I want them to be with me, and to accomplish that, I must share everything that is critical to growing the company."

Financials were shared with the teams. Slide decks for key presentations were shared—not only with the team for whom they were relevant, but with anyone who wanted to see them. In that way, the product team knew what the marketing team was doing, and vice versa. It allowed all of them to coordinate better and offer help when asked. "In many ways, it can look like overcommunicating, but that produces a much better result than filtering or withholding. The younger the workforce, the more ingrained this has become, as anyone under forty has been raised with instant information on news, entertainment, scores, data—everything! They know nothing else! Every employee had shares in our company, and as owners who were informed, they felt a passion and accountability to support the business in whatever it needed. With the Board, team, and leadership aligned on the data on the business, we could adapt, take advantage of market opportunities and quickly align to drive growth."

In any endeavor, a 70% "good decision" rate sits at the top of the expected range. If your team needs to regroup and restart at least 30% of the time, imagine how much faster they can move if they are up-to-speed as a foundation rather than as an occasional luxury.

Transparency allows companies to scale for those simple reasons.

Resourcefulness—Would you rather have an entire team of resourceful team members, or a team with full resources?

Great teams bet on resourceful people, as few teams or organizations ever feel fully resourced with enough talent, money, or time. Resourcefulness acknowledges up front that challenges almost always outweigh resources, and that there most likely will be tight time constraints as well.

In the end, finding ways to be resourceful shows up like a game, and effectively creating solutions boosts morale and saves lots of time and money. Teams move much faster when exercising resourcefulness. They also build confidence and resilience in the process. After all, they are playing and winning the game at hand!

Meet Will Hayes, CEO and President of Lucidworks, an AI platform that connects experiences throughout the entire user journey to meet customer and employee intent in the moment.

Like any tech company, Will faces technological, financial, customer, and team challenges every single day. His multiple teams are super-talented, and with a tight labor market, almost always short one or two key players. The solution: they stay open-minded, curious, and fluid. This combination results in a natural exercise in resourcefulness rather than grit.

Will noticed that at times his teams were "gritty" and saw the limitations on that value. Grit had them dig in, which often caused them to stop evolving. It kept them repetitive in a quickly changing work climate. It kept them rigid, and, worst of all, he observed blame creeping into the culture.

As Will suggested, "Blame is the death knell for growth, as once we start pointing fingers or identifying a culprit, our chances of teamwork go out the window. Instead, we strive to stay fluid, address challenges straight on—as a great chance to grow and learn rather than 'be right.' Our teams exude resourcefulness and curiosity as the ultimate tools to grow—both as individuals, and as a team. We simply make much faster progress, and

the work is much more rewarding, as we are solving challenging and often difficult problems together. Without curiosity and
resourcefulness, this would simply not occur."

How has this shown up in Lucidworks' growth? Will's reve-
nues have grown 80% per year, and Lucidworks is on track for
yet another great year. Considering all the competition in the
market, resourcefulness has proven a key ingredient in providing a competitive edge.

Resourcefulness also impacts the mood of the team. Imagine
solving super-challenging problems every day...and succeeding! You'd feel the same boost in confidence that children feel
when they finally figure out a puzzle. Boosts in confidence
create an ecosystem that attracts resourceful and curious people
and tends to weed out know-it-alls. The net effect is a positive
impact on both commercial results and the atmosphere and
mood of every player at Lucidworks.

Dissension—This is not an obvious core value, but it thrives in
many of the fastest-growing companies. How might dissension,
or the willingness to disagree, work?

You're in yet another sixty-minute meeting, where the loudest
voice in the room, or the highest-ranked leader, is pitching an
idea. In scaling companies, that process of pitching happens quite
quickly, and then the team is asked to break into small groups to
propose all of the reasons why the team should *not* act upon it.
Nothing mean. No disrespect. Nothing retaliatory. Dissenters are
encouraged, even honored, as it takes courage to dissent.

Meet Andy Pudalov, Founder and CEO of Rush Bowls. Andrew and his team clearly exercise the process of dissension in their rapidly growing company.

Seventeen years ago, Andrew was thick into a successful Wall Street career as a derivatives trader, when he quit cold turkey—the ultimate form of dissent. He, his wife, and their two small children moved to Boulder, Colorado, knowing no one and not even knowing the area. His plan? He wanted to act on his vision of eating and living well. Boulder seemed like the right place to do that, ranked high on the "healthiest cities to live" list year after year. They bought a home, and Andrew started Rush Bowls, which now boasts over a hundred franchises and successfully grew during the pandemic.

When asked who constitutes the best employees, Andrew was quick to answer: "The employees who challenge and disagree with me. I'm not the one with all of the answers. I simply set the vision, and the teams make it happen. That just does not occur if we all agree too quickly or take my view as the right one.

"In addition, the franchisees run the stores. They hold a different viewpoint and incentive than the corporate team. Those franchisees interact with every system and customer we have. If they simply agreed with every idea I had, I would lose all of that actual experience and wisdom. Even though the corporate team and the individual franchise owners do not always agree on every idea, our system works well, because we listen and take action on unconventional, quirky, and seemingly risky ideas. If not, we could not and would not grow. In the end, we often do not have consensus in most decisions, but our team knows that we can and will revisit ideas that do not work out. That helps the process of dissension thrive."

That makes Rush Bowls one of the fastest-growing franchises in the US.

Pro tip: If you want the dissension to come quickly and respectfully, require that it come in the form of a question. Rather than dissent by saying, "I think this will wreck our budgets for the year," instead ask, "How might this affect our budget?" No discussion is actually needed at that time (about the budgets), but the question in itself signals to the idea holder and the dissenter that they should ensure the idea presented is fiscally sound.

Two results kept showing up with organizations that honored, encouraged, and rewarded dissension. Teams were much more willing to focus on any ideas (quickly), and ideas started to originate from the individual and collective wisdom of the entire organization. The energetic result shows up as the entire team developing the idea, with many contributors rather than "rubber stamping" ideas because no one wants to take on the boss.

> **Two-Day-Old Sushi:** An organization cannot hold dissension well unless it pairs dissension with respect up front, and with the ability to close ranks. Without these key

ingredients, your team dissension will result in pouting for three weeks because you were on the wrong side of the vote. Dissension, in the end, signals a very healthy organization, as respect for people and ideas rests as the foundation for the process of disagreeing.

Modeling—Ever dream of being on the cover of Vogue or GQ? Well, it's not that kind of modeling. What if every person in your company modeled the highest ideals that the company stands for? Consider the home version of this powerful value. Would you be thrilled if your kids did what you do, even when you thought they did not notice? The truth stays the same for a leadership team or parents—the troops follow what you do much more than anything you say.

Recognizing that you are always modeling effective and ineffective behaviors creates the mindset to behave in ways that foster your desired outcome. Scaling teams grow fastest by modeling the effective behaviors of the leadership team—or of any member of the organization, regardless of job title or power.

For most company leaders, and parents as well, the simple recognition that they are modeling at all times for those in their care creates strong results—positively or negatively.

Meet Ben Levenbaum, Founder and CEO of Xceleration, an industry-leading provider of incentive and recognition solutions for corporations looking to drive the performance of their employees, dealers, or customers. Given the purpose of Xceleration, Ben and his team need to truly live this modeling concept!

Ben grew up in a family construction business, where work held one primary purpose: to provide for a family. Perks, engagement, recognition, and work-life balance were simply not part of the equation. As God doth hold a great sense of humor, Ben ended up building a company that espouses driving employee performance with incentives and recognition. Mind you, however, the "driving" part does not ever involve Ben and his team handing out eleventh place ribbons to poor performers on their team. Instead, they reward employees who authentically perfect high performance. Everyone must earn their rewards for his systems to work.

Here's Ben: "Our system is simple, and yet holds great depth, or else it falls flat. Every team manager takes nominations from any member of the team, for a performer who lives out one of our values at an exemplary level. The nominations turn into points that can be turned into tangible rewards. When we researched what are the best rewards to offer, that's when it became interesting. Ask an employee what they want, and typically they say, 'Just give me cash or a gift card.' But after a while, it became clear that these were not the most effective rewards to drive engagement with and maximize appreciation for their company. We found that handing out cash awards worked well enough, but after a while, a gift certificate or cash did not land so well. Imagine getting a gift card for a great steak house (because that was the prize) and you're a vegan.

"So we took it much further. Every manager and leader is now responsible for knowing their team members well enough, that when a member of their team earns an award for exemplary performance, the prize is customized to the individual. In that way, if you're all about gourmet cooking or golfing is your passion, your gift might be the best set of cookware, or a new set of golf clubs. The idea is that any gift has to hold 'trophy value'—that is, the recipient thinks of the giver every time they use the gift, and they show it off, telling friends where it came from. That system replaced cash, as far too often cash simply ended up spent on necessities.

"We found this system was both much more challenging, and simultaneously more rewarding during work from home. If you're the team leader and you have a new team member, the day-to-day activities of every team member occur primarily alone rather than in connection with your team at the office. The leaders needed to really focus on new ways to connect with and learn about what mattered to their team members, and in the end, working from home and earning an award became an even greater prize. After all, how do you exemplify one of our highest values when no one else is around?

"In the end, the only way we scale and grow is if our leaders model the highest form of each of our espoused values. If not, everything we do would appear phony or inauthentic."

Like it or not, with your kids or your team at work, you are modeling behavior. Ben and his team focus on modeling behaviors that lead to rapid growth.

Self-responsibility—Taking responsibility for your actions cuts wasted time discussing who's at fault and focuses energy on making progress. Distinguish this value as such: ***regardless of the source of any challenge (or opportunity), I will exercise 100% self-responsibility to manage or change the outcome.***

The simplest example? The IRS chooses your tax return for an audit. You could complain for weeks and weeks...or you could exercise self-responsibility in addressing the eventual clean-up.

Self-responsibility sounds like this: "Who am I that _____?" In the case of the audit, "Who am I that I have an IRS audit to manage?"

Now consider a major customer gaffe, perhaps a star employee who suddenly quits or a lawsuit at your company. Do you take full responsibility and get to work, or do you immediately assume that someone other than you made a mistake? Scaling companies expect challenges and move much more quickly with fewer meetings. How? They don't bother wasting much time on injustice, drama, gossip, or mistakes. They blame less and solve more.

Remember Doug Thede, the CEO of Lytho? They have offices in North Carolina and the Netherlands. Lytho creates software tools that help brand, and creative teams optimize their creative operations. Doug took the CEO reins at Lytho right at the start of the pandemic. He inherited great talent and potential, and as former Notre Dame coach Lou Holtz once said when a five-star quarterback threw an interception on his first pass, "Son, your potential is going to get me fired." Lytho could perform at a much higher level, given its talent.

Doug is not one to blow things up or to rant and rave. However, he knew changes were needed to re-accelerate the company's growth. While the company had a very strong culture of safety and community, the exciting growth it had enjoyed initially had slowed. People were very friendly, accepting, and polite. Everyone felt safe, welcome, and warm.

Doug knew to restart the journey to scale, Lytho needed its people to feel more than safe; he wanted them to feel responsible. He strove for an environment that would enable the company to grow rapidly, to create opportunities to advance and learn, and to enable all employees to excel and master their crafts!

The primary attribute he began to instill? Self-responsibility.

Doug started first by considering his own behavior. "When something doesn't go as planned, we naturally look for excuses outside of ourselves rather than inward. By finding blame in something or someone else, we feel better about ourselves. However, when we truly accept our role in the situation, we can better understand ourselves and how we can best proceed and improve."

For example, marketing activities at the company were struggling. Simply blaming the marketing department or its leader would be the easy response (finding blame outside of ourselves).

Rather, by asking himself, "**Who am I** that we are missing our marketing goals?", Doug was able to frame his thinking in a manner that required him to take action. "If I am not doing enough (that is, 'Who am I?'), then I had better do something more to help!"

Doug explained, "I realized that in the end, the responsibility for shifting behaviors and outcomes at Lytho fell on me, even if I was not the head of each of the teams or the holder of all of the promises. Once I took full self-responsibility, my actions shifted. I moved to action, with more conversations, more leadership, more drive. If not the CEO, then who?"

Teams and leaders started to adopt the core value and the methodology of asking "Who am I that..." questions.

As the CEO, Doug could take full responsibility for his contribution to any outcome, positive or negative. This never means that all of the credit (or blame) goes to one person (Doug, in this case), but it does mean that Doug can work to shift only himself, as the greatest form of leverage to shift the situation he wants transformed.

Notice that self-responsibility does not focus on blame, but simple acceptance of responsibility. As Doug explained, "If you make a mess, you simply clean it up. No blame. No drama. No problem. You simply move forward. When a mistake occurs, we rally, and our team regroups and moves forward. Forgiveness of mistakes is so much easier with self-responsibility as opposed to debriefs, blaming, and excuses. We just save a lot of time and energy which then gets used in making forward progress."

Not surprisingly, results began to shift with the introduction of self-responsibility into the organization. Projects stayed on schedule more often. Meetings were less frequent and shorter in length. Work began to flow more. It's no surprise that this highly effective value showed up in multiple rapidly growing companies.

> **Two-Day-Old Sushi:** Using "we" instead of "I." The term *we* often means "everyone else but me." If you're going to exercise self-responsibility, use the first-person, singular pronoun, since you are really the only person whom you have full authority over.

As a caution, if your tribe has fully bought into your current founding values, and you would like to do a culture reset, please be prepared that people may opt out. That only becomes a major issue if they opt out emotionally and mentally but stay in your employment. If they really opt out, they will leave, and that is often necessary when a founding culture needs a makeover in order to grow again.

In the end, the whole idea is to have your values be built for scale, not for beauty contestants or golden retrievers.

KEY LEARNING POINTS

1. Customized values scale companies faster, as they are tied to what becomes necessary to succeed in your commercial mission.

2. Copied values generally come from a bucket that most (slower-growing) companies use.

3. Ask three key questions to decide if your values are "expected" or useful.

4. Upgrade your values that you now see as expected.

If you're really clear about whether you are a talent company or a culture company, and you have your highest values now in place, let's consider a hiring strategy that avoids the innately human biases we tend to employ. Hiring well is a hallmark of fast-growing companies, so let's get started.

SCALING PRACTICE #5: UPGRADING YOUR VALUES TO MATCH YOUR COMMERCIAL VISION

There's an old saying in software: "Garbage in, garbage out." Your values are not garbage, but they might not be offering the catalyst for growth that is required to scale. Follow these simple steps to assess and then upgrade any values that are missing the mark.

Step #1: Give a simple pop quiz to your entire team. Ask them to state your values as listed on the website. Do this unannounced at your next team meeting and have a small prize for anyone who gets them correct. More importantly, note how many fail the quiz.

Step #2: Check your current values by asking three simple questions: 1) Could I keep a job without this value, 2) Could I have any friends without this value, and 3) Could I enter any partnerships without this value? If the answer is no to all three, that current value holds no purpose in your business or your life, as you are expected to hold it.

Step #3: Review your simple, powerful commercial vision. Is it still relevant? If so, nominate values (with your team) that contribute directly to reaching your commercial vision faster and easier. Note: Hearts, fairies, and butterfly values sound soothing but rarely help.

Step #4: Assess each proposed value first from its ability to protect you or solve big problems on your worst day; namely, use a "defense first" approach. Once a value passes the defense test, then assess the value as an offensive tool as well. Eliminate values that do not play both well. Consider the remaining values as your nominations list.

Step #5: Consider your nominations list and rank the values from most useful in accomplishing your commercial vision to least valuable.

Step #6: Consider proceeding with only one, two, or a maximum of three core values. The fewer values you hold, the more they stick in the hearts and minds of your entire team. Less is definitely more in this context.

CHAPTER 11

A HIRING METHODOLOGY THAT SCALES—TALENT OR CULTURE FIT

"When you hire people that are smarter than you are, you prove that you are smarter than they are."

—R. H. GRANT

REGARDLESS OF WHAT COMPANIES SAY, INVARIABLY THEY HIRE for both culture and talent. After most candidate interviews, the person who shows up on day one was chosen as a direct result of his or her talent, cultural fit with the company's espoused values and culture, or, most likely, some combination of both.

Here's what we also found revealing in scaling: you can clearly scale a company by hiring for talent or hiring for culture fit, but the *ad hoc* mix of the two equates to creating a no man's land.

Are you primarily a culture company or primarily a talent acquisition company? A simpler question to answer is, if you only could hire 100% for one, without regard for the other, which would it be? That's the first question to answer definitively, and answering "both" equals the largest all-you-can-eat plate of two-day-old sushi you can handle. It just will not work well, at least when it comes to your growth (or scaling) strategy.

Whether you choose to hire exclusively for talent or exclusively for culture fit, let's explore the most effective way to do so.

THE DELIGHTFUL PROBLEM WITH PEOPLE

Elie Wiesel once said, "God must love stories, because He created man."

Stories are the human currency we all share. We love to tell stories! In hiring processes, however, stories do not assist the scaling results very well.

Two versions of the same story, told by two different people, rarely match up. Herein lies the nature (and delight, sometimes) of people. Add to that dilemma the fact that human beings are inherently great judgment-making machines, and you'll see that the problem with people is that...well, we're all human.

Here's a fun way to test the theory about stories and humans. At your next gathering at your home, offer a prize for the couple whose individual stories about how they got together match each other's the most closely.

First, dismiss one member of the couple, and have the other tell his or her version of how they met. Then reverse the roles; have the partner who was initially dismissed tell how they met. Repeat the game for each couple, and then vote on which couple's stories offer the closest match. Offer another prize for the couple whose stories are most diverse, since they most likely will be more entertaining.

For a dinner party, this game is super fun and playful. For scaling, stories about candidates told by multiple players might instead present a dilemma. Hiring decisions reveal just how human we are. Your judgment and my judgment of the three finalists for a key position might look like polar opposites. Why? Pretty simple. We like and value different things, even if we agreed upon shared values in our team.

If your company is large enough to engage an HR team, another layer of complexity enters the picture, as HR is charged with nurturing, encouraging, and fostering the culture of the company—the "human" part of the company. HR's inherent bias tends to err on the side of culture fit, even if the talent required for a position is extremely specific and difficult to find. What if the hiring mandate is to consider talent as the exclusive criterion? You can see how the process might begin to fall apart at the seams with multiple interviewers with independent standards.

In short, each of us likes whom we like. We then each create a story to back up our independent judgment (call it "confirmation bias"), and the whole process can go pear-shaped rather quickly. We talk ourselves into the fact that we hired the "best fit" (based upon our story) for the team, often without the ideal talent or great culture-fit we set out to hire.

In a large percentage of companies, these decisions are made without having ever decided the mix or priority of talent over culture or culture over talent!

Rule #8: Declare to hire exclusively for talent or exclusively for culture fit. Pretending you can get the ideal mix leads to two-day-old sushi.

Now meet Joe Caruso, CEO and Co-Founder of Alliance Investors, an investor advisory firm that applies innovative methods to address the ever-changing roles of regulatory compliance, proxy advisory firms, investors, activists, and the proxy intermediaries. Joe plays in a very specialized industry where "everyone knows everyone."

Joe also holds ambitious designs on scaling—which he plans to build primarily on acquiring high-end talent. As Joe suggests, "With hiring talent and the continual acquisition of great talent, our leadership team can eventually teach and encourage a useful culture. After all, we will inherit different cultures when we acquire another firm. If we flipped to a 'culture first' scaling design, eventually our relative lack of talent cannot be overcome just because we have a strong culture. With great talent, we will unite people in a culture fit united by individual and collective talents. We can then develop and attract those who want to play with the best players in the industry. If we repel those who do not want to play on a super-talented team, we also do so knowingly. They would just be a better fit in an organization that focuses on something other than our approach."

When I asked Joe about whether or not his talent-first approach occurred at the expense of a robust culture, he was quick to add, "I can honestly say that we've never won any culture contests. But to be fair, we've never invested any time or energy in order to do so. It most likely would not help us grow. We also have not lost anyone because they did not like our culture. I suspect our culture is appropriate for what we do, and so it simply does not get discussed that much. We certainly have strong cultural values, and we focus on having those values show up in the *way* we work, more than what we talk about as a team. We value 'taking initiative' very highly, and that one key behavior connects well to our talent. It creates a dynamic where our focus on great talent essentially becomes our default culture."

Well then, does a culture-first approach shape talent—a reverse of what Joe Caruso and his team does? Would that approach affect the talent you can hire, or how your team uses their talent?

Looking at the statistics, we can say unequivocally that hiring primarily (solely?) for talent scales significantly faster than hiring for cultural fit. In comparisons between companies that scaled in the same industry, we found that talent-first companies scaled almost one year faster than culture-fit-first companies.

Specifically, the talent-first organizations got to a scaling point eleven months and eight days faster than the culture-fit-first counterparts, many of whom won awards for their culture. The talent companies simply did not rely on culture as the primary catalyst for growth.

In funding terms, this equals a savings of your monthly burn rate multiplied by 11 months and 8 days. If for no other reason, hiring exclusively for talent might save you a "crap ton" of money, or allow you not to have to fundraise for another year.

Either way, culture or talent first, your role is to get the most out of the people whom you work with. Let's explore how to do that better.

RAISING THE CHANCES WE HIRE WELL

When looking to hire, most CEOs interviewed confirmed that they had multiple people interact with candidates—either in a panel-style interview or in multiple one-on-one interviews with team members. Eventually, the multiple interviewers compared notes to decide upon the best candidates. Discussions and some form of voting ensued.

We could argue forever about whose standards were more keenly observed in a job interview with a candidate. Most often, the criteria for hiring are listed in priority order. It sounds something like this: "We want a candidate who exhibits these criteria," followed by whatever criteria are valued most.

Problem is, human beings tend to default to a version of choosing the candidate whom they *like* the best—even when "liking them" has nothing to do with the agreed-upon criteria for hiring! Listed here are some things hiring team members say in support of hiring relatively poor fits:

"I just thought she interviewed the strongest." This would imply that interviewing for jobs was the highest-valued talent for the job, which is nonsensical in many ways. Some people interview well. Others do not interview well at all. Interviewing well can create a natural likability factor that influences the decision of the hiring team. Call it unconscious bias. Numerous studies also confirm that more physically attractive candidates get hired more frequently. They receive higher starting salaries than do "less attractive" candidates! It was difficult to find even one CEO or leader who confirmed that higher starting salaries were given to better-looking people, yet in reality, it happens, and studies confirm it over and over again.

"He just seems like he would fit into the team better than the other two candidates." Is deportment, getting along, consensus, or conformity needed to succeed in the role, or is leadership, the ability to dissent, or some other quality needed to succeed? Unless conformity is the highest criterion to consider, this "fits in" idea holds giant red flags. "Fitting in" should not stand as the outstanding quality when it most likely was never declared important prior to the interview process. For a new hire taking over a struggling team, "fitting in" might be the absolute worst criterion, as big shifts, reductions in force, and an oppositional voice would be much more helpful to succeed in turning around the team.

"Hands down, the second candidate was my favorite!" This is the equivalent of voting for "most popular" in high school. It's a combination of non-specified factors, and a clear default to a general likability factor. Dangerous at best, and all too common in hiring decisions, this approach nevertheless sounds convincing.

Six months later, when the candidate is underperforming, no one recalls the hiring team overriding all of the original criteria from the interview process, nor do they recall that another candidate fit the original hiring criteria much better. The candidate everyone liked so much is not performing poorly enough to let go, but not stellar by any means. Multiply this "okay, but not great" assessment by the impact of the role in the organization (for example, C-Suite = very high impact, late-night security guard = much lower impact), and the initial hiring mistake compounds for months or even years! The cost to fix the initial poor hire is expensive, both in terms of money and in terms of the body blow to the organization for keeping or replacing the person.

Hiring is challenging, to be sure, and mostly because humans stray, and then believe their own stories...like humans are custom-built to do. Doing so definitely enters you and your team into a beauty contest for idiots, and clearly, that's not a pageant you want to win, regardless of hiring for talent first or culture first!

LET'S "GET IT RIGHT" FOR SCALE

Let's take the case where you absolutely want to hire for culture-fit exclusively. Terrific!

You know the company's highest-ranked core values, the commercial mission, and the vision, so matching and initially vetting candidates to your list of values seems pretty simple. The hiring team knows the parameters and should apply them without difficulty. Check!

Adam Grant (author of *Think Again*, among other best sellers) offers suggestions for how to stay on track toward hiring the person who fits best rather than whom you fall in love with unconsciously.

Here's how the interview process usually works:

The hiring team interviews their favorite five candidates in three-person teams. Afterward, the team assembles again to discuss and vote on whom they liked best. Here's the not-so-obvious question: Did each member of the interviewing team rate each candidate on all ranked hiring criteria?

What normally happens instead is that as part of the hiring team, I offer (and promote) my top candidate choice, and then perhaps my second candidate choice, clearly leaving the other three candidates off my list of possibilities, even if they fit the ranked hiring criteria perfectly. Why? Because I simply (and very humanly) liked two candidates better than the other three.

And why was my top candidate ranked highest? The better question: *How* was my top candidate chosen? In most organizations, the top choice is my assessment of how well the candidate met the *sum of our values*...per my judgment alone.

LIMITING HUMAN BIAS

Compliments of Adam Grant, try this instead. Have the first interviewer assess each of the five candidates for only one of the hiring requirements, and then rank those five candidates solely based upon the assigned criterion. Have the second interviewer follow the same method using only the second criterion, and have the third interviewer assess for the third criterion only. At the end of the five interviews, each interviewer has one list of the candidates, ranked one through five on how well the interviewer assessed them on one assigned criterion.

Do not share or discuss any part of the three lists or rankings until all candidates have been interviewed. Once interviews are completed, have the interviewer with the primary hiring criterion reveal his or her list, ranked one through five, followed by the second interviewer's list with the second-most important criterion, and then the third. If you like, create a scorecard as such, in order to see how a numerical ranking system changes the conversation from likability factors to the attributes and qualities required to succeed in the role.

You can always override what you observed and measured, but at least you will know you are overriding your process on purpose.

Over time, compare the hiring results using this system to the results of the system where each of the three interviewers ranks all candidates on all three hiring criteria. Do your newly hired candidates have better performance in their first thirty days than previously? If so, chances are, the difference between the person who shows up on day one and the person needed to succeed in the role has been minimized by limiting the likability factors so often inserted into the interview process.

All of us can be guilty of liking people more because they seem more like us. It's an egocentric and natural process to want people to "fit in," which is to say, match what we already have in the organization. Unless lack of diversity is the objective, the hiring criteria might dictate a different type of skill set and perhaps a different personality type to succeed. Conformity then becomes the enemy of success.

Try Adam Grant's approach, such that you avoid the beauty contest for (hiring) idiots.

Hire better. Scale faster.

KEY LEARNING POINTS

1. People tend to hire people they like rather than people that will create better results.

2. Having an agreed-upon hiring process ensures that new hires succeed more often.

3. Interviewing with multiple team members, each with one assigned hiring criterion, limits the natural human tendency to rank candidates based upon likability or personality.

GO FORTH AND SCALE!

My quest in writing this book was to find counterintuitive, predictable, and easily duplicated practices that actually scale companies better and faster. I had the help of some amazing CEOs.

The road was never straight and paved. As such, the path forward presented interesting twists, turns, and best practices that we could not have predicted when I started. The biggest surprises showed up around the structure of organizations, teams, and how they work better (or much worse) as a direct result. This finding did not become totally clear until well after a hundred interviews, as it was hidden in conversations about culture.

Culture does not equal structure, and that idea is lost on most companies. For better or worse, structure holds much more impact to shape cultures and activities in organizations than cultures actually do. CEOs spoke about both as if they were in the same realm. The big difference: culture appears as who we become as a result of what we encourage and discourage.

Structure dictates, as a catalyst, what many of those behaviors look like—positively or negatively.

As such, companies that start with a cultural mission confine their impact to the people mostly inside of their organization, as culture is "who we are" much more than "how we impact the world." Again, the confusion arises when the cultural mission starts with, "Our mission is to change the world by..." In the end, the world is not much changed by a statement that outlines who you are rather than what you will do.

The commercial vision attempts to combine both. If you want to scale, that's lesson number one: there exists only one mission, and it's commercial. Without it, no one will ever experience (at least not for long) any aspects of the great culture you have created. Commercial success will always come first, since your investors, stakeholders, customers, and team members must have it. To prove this, just think of a great product or service experience that you no longer enjoy because the company failed.

Following that theme, we attempted to separate structure from culture, because so often they look similar. They are certainly spoken about as if they are interchangeable, which could not be further from the truth. Again, catalyst versus outcome. One drives behavior at the outset, the other appears after we notice what occurred. We celebrate one and give awards for it. The other, we rarely discuss or even name. This was perhaps the most counterintuitive feature of scaling companies: they pay attention to structure *and* culture rather than culture only.

Another finding that continued to show up dealt with simplicity and singularity of values, directives, outcomes, and goals. Is it better to have five or more core values at the risk of them losing their impact, or is it more effective for scaling to pick one (at least one as the primary value) that holds a direct line toward achieving your commercial mission? We found so few companies who deployed only one core-value directive, but the ones who did all had one thing in common: they were all scaling more rapidly than their industries' pace of growth! What we heard from the CEOs who deploy only one directive is that it produced autonomy of decision-making for team members. In short, much fewer meetings were needed to discuss options because simply following the directive drove processes forward without the need for consensus or even a majority.

Simplicity might hold the key to this success. I suggest another factor that combines with the power of holding only one directive: when you have to decide on a singular "rule" or directive as the universal mandate for each team member to employ, it takes rigor to get it right. So many companies simply copied successful directives from unicorns and highflyers, only to have the directives fall flat in their own organizations. This occurs most likely because the copying requires that both companies have the same product or market, a similar size, and, most importantly, the same leadership styles in the C-Suite. "Debate and decide" showed up frequently as one of the most copied directives (from Amazon), but almost no companies we interviewed looked or felt like Amazon...so just how was this directive going to translate?

In the end, authentic core-value directives bridge structure and culture, as they tell people what to do (like a mandate). Doing that one thing starts to impact the outcomes we share, which falls more into cultural boundaries. However you keep score on whether this is structural or cultural, having to "get it right" because you limit yourself to only one directive requires rigor, lively discussion, and perhaps even some "test drives" to make sure that your directive moves you more effectively toward achieving your commercial objectives. Done well, those achievements will have positive effects on your overall culture as well.

Finally, hidden in all of this singularity and clarity, prospective team members and even customers will decide for or against you as the correct choice for them, based upon a universal directive that every person shares as a prerequisite to play on your team. This simplicity saves lots of time, energy, money, and mostly, inefficiency by hiring only people who love what you stand for—especially your clarity. Some of the most compelling one-core-value directives we found by successfully scaling companies were:

- "Do the best work of your life!"—This applies every single day. Team members love it.

- "Start with 'yes'!"—Highlighted in Chapter 7, this optimizes decision-making.

- "Love the people. Love the project!"—My own directive. If both are not true, I opt out.

Notice they all have people in common rather than strategy, product, or systems. Not to say that a super powerful one-core-value directive could not address those themes. In the end, you and your leadership team will know it when you hear it when deciding upon the most effective rule to deploy.

Surprises? There were a few, and the biggest stood out as the overestimation (statistically) of the impact of a positive or award-winning culture, as opposed to a strong talent base. The vast majority of CEOs invest an inordinate amount of time and money building and enhancing a culture that statistically scales only one in four times as well as does holding little focus on culture. Hiring for talent only, on the other hand, comprised three of the four scaling success stories.

Intuitively, this makes great sense, and sports teams generally prove it. Some super-talented teams have such a toxic locker room that they fail. Mostly, however, the better the talent on the roster, the (much) better chance at winning championships. Could it be that the culture only needs to be "good enough" as opposed to award winning?

Perhaps the focus on culture enhancement versus talent acquisition came about due to the relative shortage of extremely high-quality, *available* talent. Might it be that given relatively limited available talent, the CEOs simply decided to play in the culture game instead, since they could possibly make a difference there?

Most of the talent-first CEOs had no budgets for team off-sites, team-building activities, or cultural enhancements. Instead, they offered a workplace with very talented players and compelling challenges. They created a "playground" that engaged people such that they loved to go to work, get frustrated, solve big problems, and collaborate with their team to create results—like a kid with a thousand-piece Lego set.

That sense of play creates its own culture of sorts, and perhaps it is the most appropriate to succeed in the high-stakes game of scaling.

Thank you for joining me on the journey. Now go forth and scale!